GHOSTS IN THE SCHOOLYARD

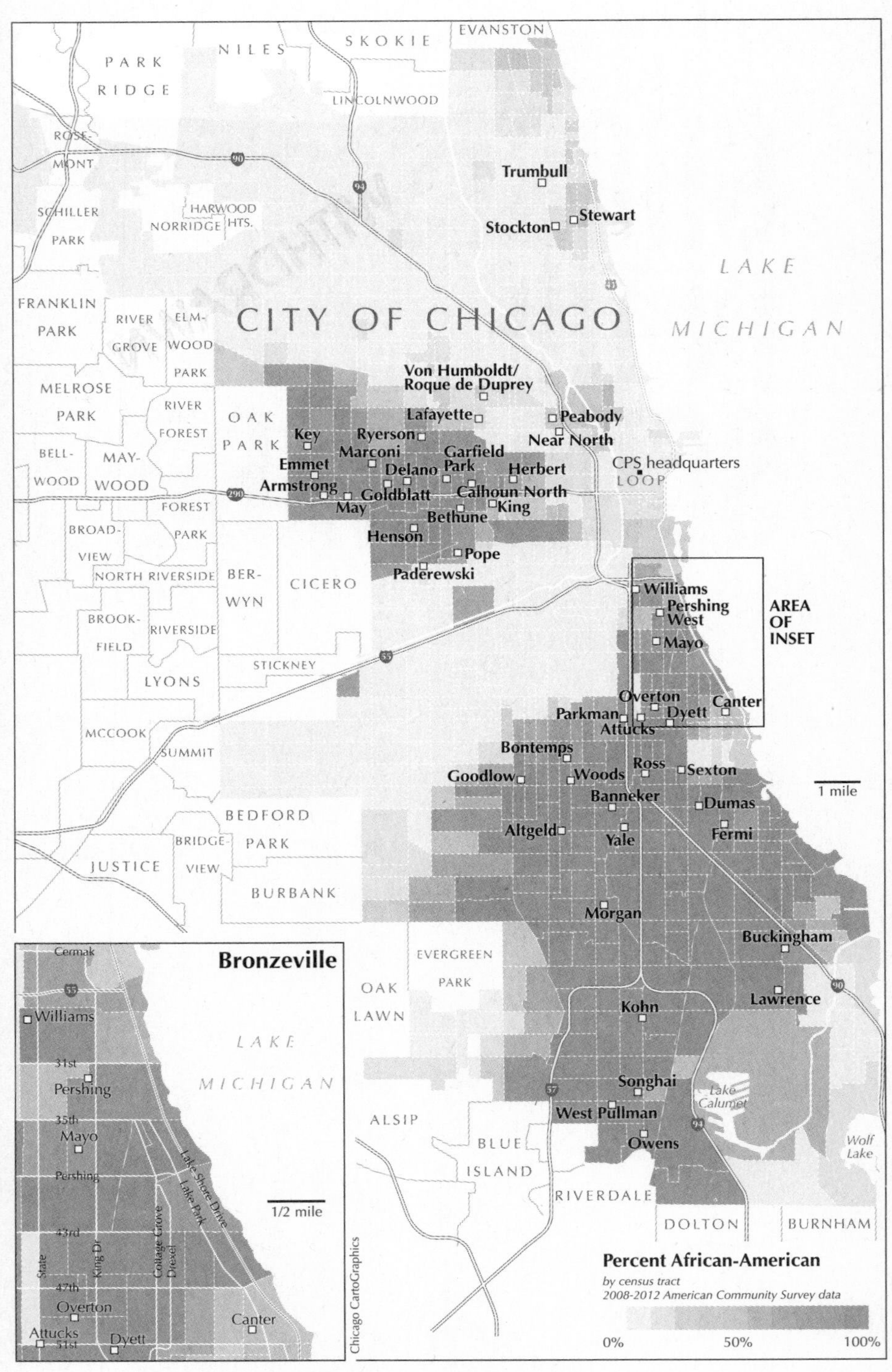

2013 School closures in Chicago.

GHOSTS IN THE SCHOOLYARD

Racism and School Closings on Chicago's South Side

EVE L. EWING

THE UNIVERSITY OF CHICAGO PRESS
CHICAGO AND LONDON

The University of Chicago Press, Chicago 60637
The University of Chicago Press, Ltd., London

Published 2018
Paperback edition 2020
Printed in the United States of America

29 28 27 26 25 24 23 22 21 20   1 2 3 4 5

ISBN-13: 978-0-226-52602-7 (cloth)
ISBN-13: 978-0-226-52616-4 (paper)
ISBN-13: 978-0-226-52633-1 (e-book)
DOI: https://doi.org/10.7208/chicago/9780226526331.001.0001

Library of Congress Cataloging-in-Publication Data

Names: Ewing, Eve L., author.
Title: Ghosts in the schoolyard : racism and school closings on Chicago's South side / Eve L. Ewing.
Description: Chicago : The University of Chicago Press, 2018. | Includes bibliographical references and index.
Identifiers: LCCN 2018010065 | ISBN 9780226526027 (cloth : alk. paper) | ISBN 9780226526331 (e-book)
Subjects: LCSH: African Americans—Education—Illinois—Chicago. | Racism in education—Illinois—Chicago. | Walter H. Dyett High School (Chicago, Ill.) | Low-performing schools—Illinois—Chicago. | Public school closings—Illinois—Chicago. | Bronzeville (Chicago, Ill.)—History—21st century.
Classification: LCC LC2803.C4 E95 2018 | DDC 370.8909773/11—dc23
LC record available at https://lccn.loc.gov/2018010065

♾ This paper meets the requirements of ANSI/NISO Z39.48–1992 (Permanence of Paper).

This book is dedicated to the educators, organizers, agitators, rabble-rousers, and dreamers who fight every day to make Chicago a city worthy of our boundless love. Thank you.

If we must die—oh, let us nobly die,
So that our precious blood may not be shed
In vain; then even the monsters we defy
Shall be constrained to honor us though dead!

—*Claude McKay*

CONTENTS

TERMS AND PEOPLE

Brizard, Jean-Claude CEO of Chicago Public Schools from April 2011 to October 2012. Brizard stepped down from his post shortly after the end of a large-scale teachers' strike that captured a great deal of local and national media attention.

Burns, Will Alderman of the Fourth Ward, which includes much of Bronzeville, from 2011 to 2016, during which time he was embroiled in the fight over Dyett High School as well as other educational issues in the city. Abruptly resigned in 2016 to become an adviser for Airbnb.

Byrd-Bennett, Barbara CEO of Chicago Public Schools from October 2012 until June 2015. Byrd-Bennett oversaw the 2013 school closures. She resigned as CEO when it was revealed that she was under federal investigation, and in October 2015 she was indicted on bribery charges for a plan in which she arranged no-bid contracts from the school district to her former mentor and employer in exchange for bribes. As of this writing, she was incarcerated in Alderson Federal Prison.

Chicago Board of Education Governing body of Chicago Public Schools, comprising seven individuals appointed directly by the mayor. In other Illinois school districts, members of the board are chosen in local elections.

CEO Chief executive officer of Chicago Public Schools, holding the position known in most other school districts as superintendent. The CEO is appointed directly by the mayor.

CHA Chicago Housing Authority, the agency that oversees public housing across the city.

Claypool, Forrest CEO of Chicago Public Schools from July 2015 until December 2017. Before his appointment as CEO, Claypool had been chief of staff to Mayor Rahm Emanuel. Before that, Emanuel appointed him as head of the Chicago Transit Authority. Claypool also served as Mayor Richard M. Daley's chief of staff from 1989 to 1993. He resigned in 2017 after the district inspector found that he had committed an ethics breach described as a "full blown cover-up."

Coalition to Revitalize Dyett A collaborative of partners first advocating for a "village" of schools designed to closely align Walter H. Dyett High School with nearby elementary schools, then protesting the school's closure after it was slated to be shut down by CPS. Coalition members include individual parents, teachers, and community members as well as organizations such as the Kenwood-Oakland Community Organization, Teachers for Social Justice, and the Chicago Botanic Gardens. Dyett is pronounced like "diet."

Daley, Richard J. Mayor of Chicago from 1955 until his death in 1976. "Old Man Daley," one of the most powerful politicians in American history, who famously oversaw many of the city's most traumatic and formative years and events with consequences that have lasted well into the current century, including the rapid rise of public housing.

Daley, Richard M. Mayor of Chicago from 1989 to 2011, the eldest son of Richard J. Daley and, like his father, immensely powerful. Initiated many educational trends and actions that laid the groundwork for the contemporary school landscape in the city. These actions include taking on complete mayoral control of the school district in 1995 and creating the "Renaissance 2010" plan to create one hundred new schools, especially through the expansion of charter schools.

Launched the "Plan for Transformation," a blueprint for demolishing and rebuilding public housing, in 1999.

Emanuel, Rahm Mayor of Chicago, elected in May 2011 after Mayor Richard M. Daley's twenty-two-year tenure. As mayor, Emanuel holds the power to unilaterally appoint the heads of both the CHA and CPS. Widely criticized after both the 2013 school closings and the police shooting of seventeen-year-old Laquan McDonald.

Kenwood-Oakland Community Organization (KOCO) A membership-based black community organizing group founded in the 1960s, based in the middle of Bronzeville and active in Dyett High School before, during, and after its planned closure. Several participants in the Dyett hunger strike were also active members of KOCO.

Receiving school (welcoming school) A school designed to receive a group of students after a nearby school is closed. Referred to as a "welcoming school" in official CPS communications.

Willis, Benjamin Superintendent of Chicago Public Schools from 1953 until 1966 (before the position was known as CEO). Criticized by black parents and civil rights leaders for policies that maintained segregation in CPS.

Introduction

We real cool. We
Left school. We
Lurk late. We
Strike straight. We
Sing sin. We
Thin gin. We
Jazz June. We
Die soon.

—Gwendolyn Brooks,
"We Real Cool"[1]

Failing schools. Underprivileged schools. Just plain *bad schools*. The fodder of *tsk-tsk, it's so sad*, and *that's why we send our kids to private school* and *we're so lucky*. They're the stuff of legend, material for inspirational movies and shocking prime-time news exposés. In Chicago they were once famously called the worst in the nation[2] by William Bennett, secretary of education under President Ronald Reagan. More recently, Illinois governor Bruce Rauner called them "inadequate," "woeful," "just tragic," and "basically almost crumbling prisons."[3] Chicago's public schools have been positioned in the nation's imagination as, at best, charity cases deserving our sympathy; at worst they are a malignant force to be ignored if you can or snuffed out altogether if you can come up with something better. In this sense Chicago is like many other urban school districts that primarily serve students of color, viewed with pity and contempt.

So in 2013, when Mayor Rahm Emanuel announced an unprecedented wave of school closures, perhaps he expected public approval. The city and the school district were facing a $1 billion budget deficit, enrollment had dropped in the district overall, and many of the schools on the list had long records of low test scores. Chicago Public Schools (CPS) first said that as many as 330 schools could be closed, then pared the number down to 129, and finally announced 54 that made the final list. Of those, 49 ultimately were slated to be closed by the end of the 2012–13 school year. Students attending these schools were assigned seats in other schools nearby.

And whatever response Mayor Emanuel and his schools chief, Barbara Byrd-Bennett, may have expected, they ultimately faced an uproar. Chicago Teachers Union president Karen Lewis publicly called Emanuel the "murder mayor." Thousands of Chicagoans took to the streets in three days of marches that proceeded from one closing school to the next. Local journalists' fact-checking reports demonstrated that the proposed closures would not come near to solving the budget problem. National commentators wrote against the proposed closures.

Emanuel was unmoved. On the day the Chicago Board of Education formally approved the closures, his office released a statement: "I know this is incredibly difficult, but I firmly believe the most important thing we can do as a city is provide the next generation with a brighter future." Byrd-Bennett, appearing before the board to push them toward a vote, called the move "imperative" and said that "we can no longer embrace the status quo."

But if the schools were so terrible, why did people fight for them so adamantly?

In the hazy cataloging of my literary mind, "We real cool" is the first line from a poem I can remember. To grow up as a schoolchild in Chicago is to know the name of Gwendolyn Brooks, most likely as the woman who wrote the short poem that starts with a group of "real cool" young people leaving school and ends with their early deaths. Brooks was the first African American to win a Pulitzer Prize, and she was the poet laureate of Illinois. But to many she will be remembered best as the bard of Bronzeville, the historically black community on Chicago's South Side that she called home. Bronzeville has been lucky in this way, blessed with an undue share of storytellers and dreamkeepers, poets and bluesmen, journalists and freedom fighters. A review of their names—names like St. Clair Drake, Ida B. Wells, and Nat King Cole—makes trying to tell a Bronzeville story seem like a foolish errand. What narrative could match their example?

In a 1983 reading, Brooks described her motivation for the poem. She was passing a pool hall one afternoon and saw a group of young boys inside. She said, "Instead of asking myself, 'Why aren't they in school?' I asked, 'I wonder how they feel about themselves.'" It is this sort of question, with its attention to agency, to speaking one's own truth, and to the presumption that a community may contain within its own wisdom the answers to its many conundrums, that has made me brave or unwise enough to try to write the chapters that follow. While they represent many hours of reading, reflection, and questioning, they also—much like Brooks's poem—result from one fundamental moment of dissonance.

Chicago is my home. I grew up here, went to public schools here, and attended college here. After I graduated, I became a public school teacher in Bronzeville. I have my fair share of startling memories from growing up in the city that shaped me, but one of the most jarring moments I ever encountered took place when I was away from home. It was 2013, I had left the classroom for graduate school, and I was visiting my father in Florida on spring break. I was alone, sitting on the edge of the bed with the door closed, my grip tightening on the glowing rectangle of my phone as I read a *Chicago Sun-Times* article listing the Chicago Public Schools that would be closing at the end of the school year. When I got to the school in Bronzeville where I'd been a teacher, I had to read and reread it and read it again to be sure I wasn't missing something. Surely this was a mistake? How could our school be on a list like this? I thought of each of my colleagues in bewilderment, thought of my principal and our students and the many hours we had all dedicated to providing a quality education. My eyes flicked upward to the statement from the superintendent, Barbara Byrd-Bennett. (In Chicago this position is referred to as the chief executive officer—the CEO.) CEO Byrd-Bennett had been quoted as saying,

> I believe that every child in every community in Chicago deserves access to a high-quality education that will prepare them for success in college, career, and in life. I believe that that's the purpose of public schools. But for too long, children in certain parts of our city have been cheated out of the resources they need to succeed in the classroom because they are trapped in underutilized schools. These underutilized schools are also under-resourced.

Two words emerged that I also read over and over: the schools, she said, were *underutilized* and *underresourced*. "But," I said aloud, "that doesn't make any sense." How could the person charged with doling out resources condemn an institution for not having enough resources? I read it again, then again, growing sadder and angrier and more confused.

And then there was the question of race. Of the students who would be affected by the closures, 88 percent were black: 90 percent of the schools were majority black, and 71 percent had mostly black teachers—a big deal in a country where 84 percent of public school teachers are white.

In the coming weeks, the explanations the district offered struck me as inconsistent at best and illogical at worst and left me tongue-tied when my fellow education researchers at Harvard asked me to clarify exactly what was happening in Chicago. The researcher in me was intrigued and puzzled, the teacher in me was mourning, and the Chicagoan in me—witness to a seemingly bottomless tradition of corruption, political abuse, and dishonesty—was skeptical. At the intersection of these identities, I became obsessed with teasing out something deeper. What role did race, power, and history play in what was happening in my hometown? Behind the numbers and the maps and the graphs, who were the people—the teachers, the children, the neighbors—who would be affected by the decision to close so many schools? And, as Brooks asked, how did they feel about themselves—about their lives, about the machinations of the city around them, about hope or despair? I chased the story to boarded-up schools and dusty library archives, to city hall and to Saturday picnics, to the empty lots where public housing projects once stood and to the brown-brick complexes where they remained. When I felt I'd answered one question, it inevitably led me to another.

Early on, when I asked a principal I knew and trusted to describe the school closure process, he took a sharp breath before calling it "a headlong rush into a spinning fan." This characterization could also describe my research process, and to orient myself

I tried to always keep an eye on the center so as to understand the rapid movement happening around me. As such, the four chapters of the book represent four different methodological approaches, all based on research conducted between January 2015 and January 2016: field observations, document analyses, review of audio transcripts, and interviews with community members. Though the approaches differ, they all aim to answer the same larger question: Why do people care so much about schools that the world has deemed to be "failing"? If these institutions are supposedly so worthless, why do people fight to save them?

This story unfolds against the backdrop of Chicago, my beautiful, hideous, deeply flawed, lovely, violent, endearing, maligned, beloved hometown. It's a city frequently noted as one of the most persistently segregated places in the nation, a towering metropolis built on a foundation of housing discrimination and violence.[4] The city is not only a setting but a character, a force acting in its own ways to influence the lives of the people who live here.[5]

This book focuses on the school closures in Bronzeville. This community on the city's majority-black South Side saw four schools slated for closure in 2013 (including the school where I'd taught), and since 1999 it has had sixteen schools either closed or entered into a "turnaround" process (where all faculty and staff lose their jobs and the school is turned over to a third party to hire new teachers). In some ways Bronzeville could be considered typical of African American communities of our era. The fortunes of the community have risen and fallen with the broader tide of social forces affecting black urban centers across the country, including segregation, housing policy, school policy, and economic trends—what sociologist William Julius Wilson calls "cycles of deprivation."[6]

At the same time, Bronzeville is special. Beginning about twenty blocks south of downtown Chicago, bounded by Lake Michigan and the Dan Ryan expressway, the region occupies a singular place as Chicago's historic hub of African American culture: the community was the destination of thousands of migrants heading to Chicago from southern states during the Great Migration and home to luminaries such as Richard Wright and Gwendolyn Brooks. (While the rest of the world might consider it something like "the Harlem of Chicago," my stubborn Second City heritage forbids me such an analogy. If anything, I might insist that Harlem is the Bronzeville of New York City.) Bronzeville is also special to me. As an African American woman writer born and raised in the city, I have long held the cultural legacy of the community as a source of identity and an inspiration—which is why I felt so fortunate to teach in a school there.

Since I have now admitted my personal (even emotional) interest in school closure as well as my preoccupation with questions of justice and social change, some readers may protest that my recounting of this narrative will not be "objective." Indeed, the story is not an objective one; I am not an objective observer, nor do I aspire to be. As critical race theorists have argued, claims to objectivity often serve as "a camouflage for the self-interest, power, and privilege of dominant groups in U.S. society."[7] What's more, such theorists would argue—and I would agree—that the experiential knowledge of people of color not only is a legitimate source of evidence, but is in fact critical to understanding the function of racism as a fundamental American social structure. So I cannot and do not aspire to tell an objective story; rather, I offer a story that is revelatory based on the experience of my own life and the lives of community members living in the shadow of history.

2013 SCHOOL CLOSINGS: WHAT WE ALREADY KNOW

There has not been a great deal of research on the CPS school closings, but what we do know helps us understand the big picture beyond Bronzeville. First, and perhaps most important, we know that the students affected by school closure tend to be some of the city's most vulnerable. Researchers have found that the closed schools served disproportionately vulnerable student populations compared with the rest of the district, including more low-income students, more students who moved often, more students who had repeated a grade at least once, and more students who received special education services.[8]

In 2009 researchers conducted an analysis to see whether students received academic benefits after their schools closed. After all, this was, and still is, a common argument presented in favor of school closings: Won't the students end up at superior schools and so be better off than at their old schools? As it turns out . . . not really. Researchers compared 5,445 CPS students aged eight and older whose schools were closed from 2001 to 2006 with a group of students at similar schools.[9] There was no real change in these students' math or reading outcomes, and they were just as likely to be held back or referred for special education. But worse, the authors found that students attending closed schools had experienced a drop in academic achievement during the year *before* the school actually closed, amid the turmoil of the announcement. Once students and teachers found out their schools were closing, it was hard to stay academically on track for the rest of the year. News of school closings hurt students' performance, and moving to new, supposedly better schools didn't help.

So what happened after the students were relocated? The results varied depending on the quality of the new school. Students who moved to the city's lowest-performing schools saw losses in reading and math, while students who enrolled the city's top-performing schools saw small gains. But the first group—those relocated to schools in the bottom quarter of test score rankings—was much larger. Of the displaced students, 42 percent went to the lowest-ranked schools, and only 6 percent ended up in top-ranked schools.[10] And of that small group, most students had to travel a significant distance to get to their new schools—an average of 3.5 miles.

In other words, the argument that school closings can be good because students will end up in better schools is theoretically possible. But research suggests that this happens only for students who find themselves relocating to top-tier schools, which turns out to be a very small percentage, and those children on average have to go very pretty far from home to get to the new school. The reality is that students who experience school closure end up at new schools that are not thriving academically, so they don't receive any boost or improvement in their education. This makes sense, because the history of segregation and inequality has left struggling schools largely clustered together across the landscape, meaning that students leaving a school facing challenges are likely to end up in an equally challenged school close by.

Perhaps informed by these findings, during the 2013 closings CPS officials decided that for each closing school there would be a higher-performing "welcoming school" for students to attend—though in practice parents did not *have* to enroll their children in this designated receiving school. After the 2013 closings, two-thirds of CPS students attended their designated receiving schools, one-quarter enrolled in other traditional public schools, and the rest enrolled in either charter schools or magnet schools.[11]

What did the parents of those children who were displaced by school closings have to say? They reported that school closings had a negative effect on their children overall; they criticized the academic offerings, extracurricular options, and resources of their children's new schools and said that school closings severed their relationships with school overall. They also said the schools that closed had deep personal meaning beyond being an academic resource, leaving children with a sense of loss. Parents reported feeling excluded from their children's new schools; they felt "powerless" during the closing process, as though district leaders "didn't really care" and "didn't give the parents or the staff a chance" to defend their closing schools. At their new schools, many parents felt alienated from events, meetings, and opportunities to participate or volunteer at school or were just generally discouraged.[12]

Last, parents described an overall distrust toward CPS, were critical of the stated reasons for school closings, and wanted a voice in CPS decisions. Many parents interviewed openly expressed their view of the racism inherent in the closings, stating that CPS decision makers "don't care about African American communities. They don't care if we get an education." Others were suspicious of the motives behind school closings, believing they were designed to expand charter schools and displace low-income residents to the periphery of the city or beyond its borders. In sum, these parents presented a version of events that challenges the dominant narrative from CPS.

RACE TALK: THINGS SAID AND UNSAID

Our culture has an odd relationship with race: it structures every aspect of American social life, but in ways that can often seem invisible and undetected. Like an electrical current running through water, race has a way of filling space even as it remains invisible. In the news and the media we talk about it constantly—especially during election seasons—but in our everyday lives many people are uncomfortable discussing race and racism, especially with people from different backgrounds.

Much of this book will explore the role of race in the school closure decisions and their aftermath. But before we can understand whether school closings are racist, we have to understand what racism *is*, and those who support or oppose school closings seem to disagree on that front. CPS CEO Barbara Byrd-Bennett, when accused of racism, said that school closure proposals were tied to "demographic changes, and not race" and called such accusations personally offensive to her as a woman of color. Chicago Teachers Union president Karen Lewis, on the other hand, called the school closings racist and classist. To those two black women, does "racist" mean the same thing?

For many, the word racism conjures up images from history: *whites only* signs on water fountains, burning crosses, angry mobs screaming at the Little Rock Nine or at Ruby Bridges. Others may recognize racism in the present, but only when it is overt: the harsh words of those who would see all Muslims banned from the United States, or Donald Trump referring to Mexican people as "criminals" and "rapists." But in the decades since Jim Crow, racism has become less obviously bound to formal institutions and laws, making it more difficult to identify. Instead, we see *laissez-faire racism*, a form of discrimination that does not depend on the law, but instead "relies on the market and informal racial bias to re-create, and in some instances sharply worsen, structured racial inequality."[13] We might think of this form of racism as being like a mechanical toy: you wind it up and it goes off on its own. In the United States, the racist structures that *were* inscribed in law generations ago—when "separate but equal" was perfectly legal—established the framework for the way our society currently functions.

Often, when people talk about "racism" they are using the term to refer to a set of ideas or personal values. In their view, racism is a disease that afflicts some individuals and causes them to discriminate against others just because of the way they look.[14] This version of racism is familiar from everyday discourse; we hear people say things like "I have no racism in my heart" or "How can I be racist? My best friend is black!" This characterization views racism as something that lives in an *individual*—that has to do with one's beliefs and opinions. It is often complemented by the idea of *color-blindness*, exemplified by the common claim that "I don't even see race" or "everyone is the same to me—I don't care whether they're black, white, red, yellow, green, or polka-dot." Those who use such language are making several implicit claims: *I'm not a racist. Racism means seeing people differently and treating them differently. I see everyone the same.* This perspective locates racism within individuals and what we "see." It also suggests that even to acknowledge racial difference is a form of racism; this creates a conflict, since those harmed by racism require an acknowledgment of their racialized status in order to have a conversation about injustice. (For example, to talk about the contemporary legacy of slavery, the genocide of indigenous people, or the internment of Japanese Americans, one needs to admit that we are in fact *not* all the same.)

For sociologists—as well as for many activists and others—it is more accurate to think of racism as a set of structures organizing the way society works. This view characterizes racism as something that lives not in individuals, but in *systems*—in the fabric of American society. Through this lens, what is in one's "heart" does not matter. Rather, the question becomes how our society follows a pattern, churning out different outcomes for different people in ways linked to race. This happens with or without the consent, awareness, or intentions of individuals.

One metaphor we can use to understand these two ideas is riding a horse. Many people believe racism is like a skilled equestrian's choosing, through decisions and commands, to go faster or slower, to jump a fence or avoid an obstacle, to follow a certain route or not. However, thinking structurally, we can understand that racism is more like a merry-go-round. You may be going up, down, and around, and you might feel as if you're riding a horse, but the machine is functioning with or without you. From this viewpoint we can come to see acts of racism not as the result of individuals' being socially deviant (as suggested by phrases intended to explain acts of racism, such as "there are just some sick people out there"), but as perfectly normal and predictable because they are built into the social system.[15] Put simply, racism is as American as apple pie.[16]

In other words, the question of whether something is racist may be more complicated than it appears on the surface. Throughout this book we will see instances where something racist occurs, but not because an individual is hurling epithets or explicitly trying to harm black people. Rather, these events and policies are racist because they result in the systematic disenfranchisement of black people and harm to black children—regardless of intent—and because they are bound up in the perpetuation of historical policies rooted in more explicit racism. And this, in part, is why people fight so hard for their schools: because the fight is actually about a great deal more than just one building.

BUT WHY DO PEOPLE CARE ABOUT THESE FAILING SCHOOLS?

Why do people care about these "failing" schools? I address this question in four chapters, each exploring a different aspect of school closure in Bronzeville. For starters, the issue actually is not even the school; it's a history that goes undiscussed, a history that provokes justifiable anger and mistrust. People care because in some cases they don't view the schools as failing. And they care because the consequences of the closure are emotionally devastating.

In chapter 1, I tell the story of Dyett High School, whose impending closure inspired community members to lead a monthlong hunger strike. In chapter 2 I discuss the history of segregation and public housing in Bronzeville to dig deeper into the claim that Bronzeville schools are "underutilized." In chapter 3 I use public hearing transcripts to let us listen in during 2013 as community members, parents, teachers, and students fought to keep their schools open. Finally, in chapter 4, as a way of understanding community members' emotional responses to school closure I present a theory I call institutional mourning—the idea that we can mourn lost institutions just as we mourn lost people.

And along the way we hear from people like Martin,[17] a young man who has seen both his grammar school and his high school close, as he discusses the threat school closure poses to community memory and legacy—all intertwined with race. "As you're getting older," he says, "and you're listening to these stories, at some point you still gotta move on and you can't . . . you're not going to remember everything your parents told you. So that's how you get black history to go away. That's how you get black history to go away." Here, standing on the shoulders of the many storytellers who have made Bronzeville's reputation the stuff of legend among black Chicagoans, is where I hope to intervene. I began this inquiry to understand something that confounded me, but in the end I hope to have documented the injustice and resilience and desire and agony of this singularly important community. I hope I can keep black history from going away. I hope to help us understand, and remember.

1 *What a School Means*

> Cause everybody dies in the summer / wanna say your goodbyes, tell 'em while it's spring / I heard everybody's dying in the summer / so pray to God for a little more spring.
> —Chance the Rapper, "Pusha Man (Paranoia)"

> And finally, need I add that I who speak here am bone of the bone and flesh of the flesh of them that live within the Veil?
> —W. E. B. Du Bois

For an August day in Chicago the weather is unseasonably cool, and many of the people sitting in the park have blankets draped over their laps or around their shoulders. In many ways this looks like any family gathering in Washington Park—older faces and younger faces in a circle of fabric lawn chairs and coolers, chatting amiably. But rather than pop, picnic food, or snacks, many of the coolers are filled with infused water or high-nutrient juices. Thermoses of hot broth are propped against a tree. And there are people here you wouldn't see at a family picnic: visitors from across the city, reporters and photographers from across the country. Worried nurses flit from person to person. No music is playing. Sometimes folks laugh and joke cheerfully; other times they look off into space, exhausted.

Behind it all a tremendous black building looms, its windows dark. And that is the reason these people are here—not for any family reunion or summer gathering, but in the name of this shuttered building, Walter H. Dyett High School. They are not picnickers, they are hunger strikers. And they are putting their lives on the line in hopes of seeing their vision for this school become reality.

Why do people fight for schools like this? While the Dyett hunger strike would rise to public prominence as one of the most visible examples of community members fighting to save a school, it is hardly the only one. Across the country, school stakeholders who are culturally and geographically very different have waged notably similar battles to get their schools off district chopping blocks. In Detroit in 2017, hundreds of parents and community members rallied in front of the state of Michigan's offices to protest the closing of schools that others referred to as "consistently failing" and "the worst of the worst."[1] In Shreveport, Louisiana, in 2011, parents held meetings and circulated a petition to save Blanchard Elementary, which the district called "small," "lacking," and "old."[2] In Austin, Texas, in 2016, parents organized high turnouts at community meetings and picketed to fight the district's closure of ten schools it said were in poor physical condition and underenrolled.[3] In Dyett's case the media declared that "by just about any definition [the school] has failed."[4]

To outside observers—concerned neighbors and friends, informed citizens reading about education issues in the news or seeing these protests on television—it may be hard to reconcile these characterizations. If the schools are *small, the worst, lacking*, and so on, why is anyone fighting for them? This question may be amplified by the image of public schools we see and hear in the media, from *A Nation at Risk* to *Dangerous Minds*. As someone who attended public schools and later taught in one, I can't count how many times a stranger remarked to me in casual conversation that I was an "angel" or a "saint" because public schools were "just so bad," with no clear reasoning about why or in what way.

This chapter tells the story of one group of people fighting to keep a school open—and, moreover, to see it reflect their vision for their community and their children's education. We see that this community's choice to resist a school's being characterized as "failing" is in fact about much more than the school itself: it is about citizenship and participation, about justice and injustice, and about resisting people in power who want to transform a community at the expense of the people who live there.

THE DYETT TRADITION

So much of black life in Chicago happens in Washington Park that if you are African American, even if you are from the West Side or (like me) the North Side, it is hard not to find yourself there at least once each summer. The African Festival of the Arts, the Bud Billiken Parade, and family barbecues all find a home in the massive park. Sitting at the southern edge of Bronzeville, it covers 367 acres landscaped by Frederick Law Olmsted, the architect most famous for his design of New York City's Central Park. At the northern end of the park, facing Fifty-First Street, a low building of black glass looks out over a broad expanse of grass. In summer 2015 the building is empty, but the flag still flies above it. The sign still says "Welcome to Walter H. Dyett High School" in black against a yellow background, bright against the backdrop of the dark building and Chicago's more often than not gray weather. But no doors are open. No teenagers gather to talk or to run, to flirt or gossip or tease, to play football or scramble for forgotten homework or do the things teenagers do. Walter H. Dyett High School is closed.

Not many schools are named after teachers, so it is notable that this building is as much a living monument to Walter H. Dyett as it is an educational institution. It is also notable that this man, arguably the most renowned and respected educator ever to emerge from Bronzeville—a community famous for its musical venues and figures—was a bandleader and music teacher.

Walter Henri Dyett was born in 1901 in Saint Joseph, Missouri. His mother was a pianist and soprano vocalist, and his father was a pastor in the AME church. Dyett began his musical life as a violinist after his family moved to California; as a student at Pasadena High School, he became concertmaster of the orchestra and also played clarinet, bassoon, and drums. After graduating in 1917, he attended the University of California at Berkeley, where he was first violinist in the school's symphony orchestra while he completed his premed studies. In 1921 Dyett received a scholarship to the Illinois School of Medicine and moved back to Chicago to pursue his studies. However, his mother and sister, already living there, needed financial help, and he took on work as a musician to support his family. In a curriculum vitae dating from 1960, Dyett described the early days of this work: "One year violinist in Erskine Tate's Vendome Theatre Orchestra playing the silent pictures and stage presentations along with Louis Armstrong and other now internationally known musicians. Transferred to orchestra leader in the Pickford Theatre—one of the Vendome chain—and remained until talking pictures came in and orchestras went out." He next became youth music director at a church, then a private teacher of violin and music theory. Finally, in 1931 Dyett began the work for which he would become beloved: he became a music teacher at Phillips High School in Bronzeville. When Phillips was relocated in 1936 and renamed Du Sable High School (after the city's founder, the Haitian Jean Baptiste Point du Sable), Dyett went along to the new school.

FIGURE 1 Dyett (far right) addressing the Du Sable High School band, December 22, 1954. Source: Walter Henri Dyett Papers, box 7, folder 89, Vivian G. Harsh Research Collection of Afro-American History and Literature, Chicago Public Library.

Tribute concerts, memorials, and articles about Dyett often cite his influence on the Bronzeville musical legends who were his students, such as Von Freeman and Nat King Cole. But while these figures loom large in history, they were far outnumbered by the thousands of average Bronzeville teenagers who discovered a love of music through his schoolwide concerts and community initiatives during his thirty-eight years as a teacher (fig. 1).

Dyett was intentional about the pedagogical principles he brought to his work. He explained them in detail in his 1942 master's thesis for the Chicago Musical College, which explored methods for teaching the fundamentals of rhythm to high school students and argued that music education could help students develop joy and discipline. "The student learns from experience," Dyett argued, "and these experiences must be enjoyable ones if the proper interest necessary for this learning is to be motivated and sustained." In another chapter he wrote, "If, in our music classes, we can kindle a spark which will inspire the students to be satisfied with only the best work that they are capable of performing, this development will surely be carried over into whatever field of endeavor they may choose for a vocation." In a 1969 letter to the musicians' union celebrating Music Appreciation Week, Dyett echoed the importance of such disciplined determination to do one's best work: "The world today calls for dreaming possibilities and developing these possibilities into live realities and actualities. Creativity development comes by: becoming receptive to ideas—welcoming new ideas; by being experimental . . . by accepting the opportunity to do more; by asking how can I do more—how can I improve the quality of my performance—how can I do better?"

These principles were to serve as the core of the school that would bear Dyett's name—a middle school with the motto "develops individuality, encourages responsibility, and provides opportunity."

When Walter H. Dyett Middle School was dedicated in 1975, the program reflected the scope of Dyett's influence on his students:

> Few musicians, living or dead, have brought music into the lives of so many young people and made them a part of the world's music. . . . He was the complete musician: an artist who could teach, a musician's musician, a student's inspiration, able tutor, and friend. . . . [H]e personally taught or supervised the music education of some 20,000 young people. He brought music appreciation and serious awareness of good music to another half million youth through his activities as a conductor of bands and orchestras in school assemblies and public programs and concerts. . . . Dyett was well known for his practice of sharing his

> baton and podium with promising young musicians and many of them are continuing the "Dyett tradition," as they enrich school systems in Chicago and elsewhere as music educators, or in the music profession as performers or entertainers.

The decision to name a school after Dyett—a local titan who dedicated his life to young people not on a citywide or national stage but in one specific community, someone who in sharing his passion and his care with generations of students did what all teachers set out to do—appears to be a tacit way of celebrating the community itself. It is a way of saying that a life lived in the service of Bronzeville is a notable life, and that the legacy of someone so dedicated to the community is worth memorializing with something important. Dyett, like many all over the intensely segregated city, was an all-black school, and its daily social happenings took place within what renowned sociologist W. E. B. Du Bois called "the Veil"[5]—the border of an all-black world. In a society that for centuries has drawn absolute boundaries between black people and white people—social boundaries, legal boundaries, economic boundaries, physical boundaries—black social life under conditions of segregation has developed its own reason and rhythm. The Veil, derived as it is from the painful constraints of slavery and Jim Crow and their aftermath, can be cruel. But behind the Veil, Walter H. Dyett, a man whose life could have been seen as ordinary, was honored as a hero.

"CHOICE" AND CHANGE

In 2000, Dyett Middle School faced a major upheaval. CPS introduced plans to convert Dr. Martin Luther King Jr. High School, a little more than a mile away, into a college preparatory school, with a selective admissions system based on test scores and grades rather than open enrollment. King would receive a multimillion dollar renovation, and students from all over the city would be able to attend—if they could meet the stringent admissions requirements. The move was part of CPS's creation of a suite of "selective enrollment" schools designed to attract the top academic (and top socioeconomic) tier of the city's high school students through a rigorous curriculum and high-end facilities. The transition also meant that if their test scores did not make them eligible to attend the new, selective King, students in the area would need a new place to go—so Dyett would be changed from a middle school to a high school. Neighborhood residents were not happy with this plan. One parent of a King student expressed frustration that the $20 million to be invested in the school's renovation was nowhere to be found when the school's enrollment was based on neighborhood attendance boundaries. Another community member lamented that young people in the area would be "shipped out of their neighborhood in order to turn King into a magnet school," suggesting that this ostensibly public school would no longer be public at all:

> If something is public, then ain't I the public? Aren't these kids who are being put out of King High School and going over there to Dyett [High School], [which is like] a factory, aren't they part of the public? How can you have a public school and then say everybody in the public can't go to it? That's what I think. It's a bunch of hogwash. . . . You don't make no magnet school with my money. I did not tell you to do that, and I don't want King to be a private school in my neighborhood. If it's public, I want you to do the best that the public can get right over there for the people in this community.[6]

The development of selective enrollment schools was just one piece of what would, over the following decade, become an expansion of "choice" within CPS. No longer would students necessarily attend the schools in their immediate areas, as they had done for generations. Instead, new schools appeared or were converted across the South Side, with varying purposes and admissions policies: several charter schools, a military academy, a technology school, an international school, and others now dotted the landscape. This evolution of the district into a "portfolio"[7] of options parents are expected to choose among was part of a nationwide trend that deemphasized local or community-based schools in favor of thinking of each city as a marketplace of options. While choosing the best option from a menu of possibilities is appealing in theory, researchers have documented that in practice the "choice" model often leaves black families at a disadvantage. Black parents' ability to truly choose may be hindered by limited access to transportation, information, and time, leaving them on the losing end of a supposedly fair marketplace.[8] Further, this shift in Chicago occurred in tandem with a broader conversation about a city in flux—a city that, in order to claim a place as a "world class" urban center, was dead set on transforming its neighborhoods to make them more attractive to white residents at the expense of a displaced black populace.[9]

Meanwhile the school "right over there" languished. While enrollment at Dyett varied over the decade, its student numbers eventually began to decline. By 2011 only 19 percent of the students within Dyett's attendance area were enrolled in the school.[10] Most families in the neighborhood were no longer choosing Dyett, opting to send their children elsewhere (fig. 2).

On November 30, 2011, parents of Dyett students received a letter from CPS CEO Jean-Claude Brizard. It began,

> *Dear Parent or Guardian:*
>
> As Chief Executive Officer of the Chicago Public Schools (CPS), nothing is more important to me than making sure your child

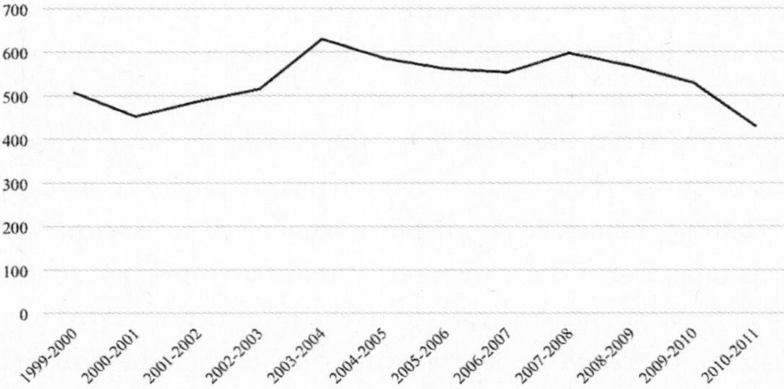

FIGURE 2 Dyett enrollment, 1999–2011. Source: Chicago Public Schools, School data, 2016.

is getting access to a high quality education. My team is dedicated to ensuring that every child in every community can be successful in the classroom and graduate ready for college and career—which is why I am writing to you today.

There are too many schools in Chicago failing our children. Across the District, only 7.9% of 11th graders last year tested ready for college, while achievement gaps for African American and Latino students remain in the high double-digits. As adults, we all have a responsibility to make sure that we are putting the academic needs of our children before all else. To do so requires some very difficult but necessary choices to boost the academic achievement of our kids.

For too long, Dyett High School (Dyett) has been one of the schools not meeting the needs of its students. Over the last few years, Dyett has been a chronically underperforming school with a graduation rate that is far below that of other schools in its area and is among the lowest academic scoring schools in the district. This is why we are proposing today, after a very lengthy and thoughtful process, to phase-out Dyett. This means

> that current ninth, tenth, and eleventh grade students would continue to attend Dyett, but the school would not enroll new students next school year.

The letter went on to say that Dyett would continue phasing out one grade each year, with the closure completed by the 2014–15 school year (when only seniors would remain).[11]

Brizard told the local news media he would prefer to send new teachers and resources to Dyett and other schools proposed for phaseout rather than shutting them down. But he felt that Dyett was beyond such measures and that sending more resources would be pointless. "There are some schools that are so far gone that you cannot save them. There's got to be some hope left in the building for you to be able to turn a school around."[12]

So far gone. With these matter-of-fact words, Brizard painted Dyett as a failing school, an institution beyond redemption. We see this language, the archetype of the "failing school," frequently in our society. The notion that the school is a failure creates a supposedly urgent space for the public to support policymakers in whatever drastic methods may be needed to address the failure. In this sense the rhetoric of the "failing school" serves as a bogeyman or as political theater, a mythology intended primarily to frighten us not into action, but into unflinching agreement with whatever action those in power opt to take.[13] Why should anyone bother to defend a failure?

As it turned out, there was at least one group who were not satisfied with Brizard's characterizing Dyett as an unsalvageable failure. And they were ready to take him on, using a variety of tactics. The phaseout nature of the plan meant there was a window of a few years for teachers, students, parents, and community members to organize in hopes of reversing the board's decision. In 2012 they staged sit-ins and several were arrested for peaceably refusing to leave city hall.[14] Thirty-six students filed a federal civil rights complaint with the US Department of Education alleging that closing Dyett reflected racially discriminatory practices:

> Throughout Dyett's entire history, the Board has demonstrated a disregard for the student body. The Board has deprived our school of resources, and undermined numerous promising attempts by our community to improve the school. What was the Board's response when, as late as 2008, we had the largest increase in students going to college in all of Chicago Public Schools? What about in 2009, when we had the largest decrease in student arrests and suspensions? Disregard and disinvestment. We are now a school with only 1 counselor, no assistant principal and have lost several quality teachers. We are a school where one our most successful programs, AVID, which prepared many of us for college was cut last year. As explained below, this may very well have been because the Board knew long ago that it would close Dyett, and felt that investing resources in us was unwise. This history of neglect impacts us—it sends us the message that the Board does not think we are worthy of investment and that our education is somehow less important than the education of our peers around the city.[15]

In 2013 several groups came together and formed the Coalition to Revitalize Dyett, a partnership between community organizers, representatives from the Chicago Teachers Union and Teachers for Social Justice, professors from the University of Illinois at Chicago, and organizational partners such as the Du Sable Museum of African American History and the Chicago Botanic Gardens. The Coalition developed a plan to keep Dyett open, which it submitted unsolicited to new CEO Barbara Byrd-Bennett (Brizard was gone by then, after only seventeen months in the position). They proposed that Dyett be a high school focused on "global leadership and green technology," with a focus on environmental sustainability, social justice, and twenty-first-century careers, to be known as Dyett Global Leadership and Green Technology High School.[16] This proposal was an extension of a project already in the works before news of Dyett's phaseout was announced: a plan for a "Bronzeville Global Achievers Village" that would align Dyett with local elementary schools. The "village" plan was based on community outreach to local parents over the course of eighteen months and was intended to create a sense of stability and solidarity in a part of the city rocked by years of school closures.[17]

For Dyett's supporters, the official assessment of the school as a failure was unacceptable, the latest manifestation of a long-running pattern of abandonment and disregard. "The Board's policy of closing one school after another in this hot real estate market has disrupted the lives of countless African American children and set back their educational opportunities. Some of us at Dyett and Price have been moved two or more times," wrote the students in their Title VI civil rights complaint.

> No school with disproportionately white enrollment would face this. As they are being pushed across gang boundaries, our friends and relatives will once more be placed at risk—their physical safety is being jeopardized. The closings are traumatic. Dyett has served as a stable institution in our lives, something that means a lot to all of us, but especially to the 30% of Dyett students who are homeless. It is inexcusable to send our community through yet another disorienting experience—and the only possible reason for this repeated forced removal into new and strange schools is that, being poor and African American, we are viewed as expendable.[18]

For this reason the word revitalize in the group's name was significant, since it countered the failing school label. By its very nature, "revitalize" signals something that was once lively and has the potential to be lively again, something that has fallen on hard times but can thrive if you fill it with energy—with vitality. Revitalize suggests that something is not perfect but can be better.

It was a Tuesday in August 2014—a year before Dyett was scheduled to be closed for good—when I heard that members of the Coalition would be holding a sit-in in front of the office of Alderman Will Burns.[19] They were demanding that Burns meet with them to discuss their proposal to keep Dyett open. I knew where the alderman's office was—35th and King Drive, four blocks from where I used to teach, right across from the King Branch of the Chicago Public Library where I led occasional study sessions for my students. I jumped in the car, stopping at the grocery store in Lake Meadows to pick up some fruit and bottles of water to take to the sit-in. I spent the afternoon in a folding chair, shifting periodically as the sun moved, drinking water and chatting with an older woman who told me stories of her grandfather's store in Mississippi, her move to Chicago when she was twelve, and her traveling back to the South every summer of her childhood. The alderman never emerged.

Two months later I saw a headline that made my eyes widen. "CPS reverses course, says Dyett to reopen in 2016 as neighborhood high school." The first three words were stunning enough. CPS reverses course? About a school closure? I'd never heard of such a thing. I kept reading:

> CPS officials made the surprise announcement Friday that they want proposals for a new, open enrollment neighborhood high school to be located at Dyett High, the Washington Park school

> that is in the last year of being phased out. . . . CEO Barbara Byrd-Bennett said in a press release that she looks forward to working with the community. CPS spokesman Bill McCaffrey said the Dyett request-for-proposals to run the school will be separate from a request for new charter schools, which also will be issued in December.[20]

Everything about this news awed me. I had seen Byrd-Bennett and other CPS officials remain steadfast in their decisions even in the face of tremendous protest from thousands of teachers and students, apparently without a second thought regardless of the scale of the criticism. Bronzeville had lost school after school in the past decade, even before the citywide mass closures of 2013. Charters had expanded, and schools had been subjected to the "turnaround" process, but never had I heard of a school having its fate sealed only for the decision to be undone. Furthermore, the district was seeking community input and soliciting open proposals not for a charter or contract school, but for a neighborhood school? I was astounded, and tremendously impressed at the impact of the community members I had met that day in August. Through their resolve, they had opened the way for this seemingly impossible opportunity; the article described the rallies, sit-ins, and civil disobedience leading to arrests that had taken place since the phaseout of Dyett was first announced. Could Dyett, I wondered, become a model for the future of Chicago's closed schools? Could it be a demonstration proof illustrating that it was possible for a community to undo a top-down decision and remake a school to reflect the desires of its residents? Could this proposal process serve as the pattern for a new form of engagement between the district and members of the community? I was excited, hopeful, and curious. When I learned the date of the public meeting where community-created proposals for a new Dyett would be presented and discussed, I eagerly cleared my schedule in anticipation.

"WE ARE SPEAKING. WE HAVE SPOKEN."

It is a weighty irony that the meeting to consider the proposals for a new Dyett was held at King College Prep. Next to it, the windows of Florence B. Price Elementary School are dark. That school's closure was announced in the same year as Dyett's but completed at the end of that school year. Piles of chairs and books are visible through the windows, and through the cloudy glass of one classroom one can just make out an American flag. Florence B. Price, like Walter H. Dyett, was a groundbreaking musician: a classical composer who became the first African American woman to have a composition played by a major orchestra when the Chicago Symphony Orchestra debuted her *Symphony in E Minor* in 1933. Indeed, this is a very musical block: Price Elementary sits at the corner of Drexel Boulevard and the honorary Muddy Waters Drive, named for the legendary icon of Chicago blues. The grass along Drexel looks especially green after the recent rain. I cross a wide concrete expanse to reach the doors of King, above which a mosaic reads "THROUGH THESE PORTALS AWAITS YOUR FUTURE." My future has to wait a few minutes, since the doors are locked.

Eventually I was admitted and found a seat near the front of the auditorium. The meeting format was straightforward. There were three proposals for consideration, and representatives for each proposing group would have twenty minutes to present their ideas for how the new Dyett should operate. Those presentations would be followed by an open comment period; participants were permitted to speak only if they had signed up as they entered the meeting and would have two minutes to comment after being called to the microphone. A court reporter and a note taker would record comments. "There will not be a question and answer period, because that's not the goal for this meeting," said the district representative overseeing the proceedings. Contact information for CPS and for each of the presenters was on the back of a handout, and attendees were directed to ask any questions later, using that information to "engage with them directly." The proposals were also available to view or download on a CPS website, along with a rubric for evaluation.

What was less clear was what was supposed to happen after the meeting and how the decision would be made. How would the community feedback from this meeting be integrated? This community meeting was to be followed by an official hearing, after which the board would make a decision. Would their decision incorporate input from other sources such as the alderman or the mayor? This was unclear, and no location was yet set for the hearing. Further complicating matters, CEO Barbara Byrd-Bennett, who issued the request for proposals in the first place, was no longer in her position. She went on leave in April amid a federal investigation into a no-bid contract and had finally resigned just two weeks before this proposal meeting (Byrd-Bennett has since been found guilty of federal charges related to bribery). What role would the interim CEO, or Byrd-Bennett's replacement, play in the future of Dyett?

During the meeting, the Coalition to Revitalize Dyett offered its proposal. It began with short videos of community members' and students' testimonials in support of the Coalition's plan. Speakers went on to explain the two prongs of the curriculum described in the proposed school's name: global leadership and green technology. In this school, students would learn urban agriculture techniques that would allow them (in partnership with the Chicago Botanic Gardens) to sell fresh produce in the community, and they could take the courses needed to become certified as building planners by LEED (Leadership in Energy and Environmental Design). Solutions for issues like global climate change and environmental racism, the team argued, "depend in part on students learning to connect their academic studies in school to the realities outside. That's why the new Dyett has roots in the community and branches out to the world beyond." This community responsiveness was explained further in the proposal:

> The Design Team believes that this proposal speaks directly to the needs as expressed by the Bronzeville community that we describe above in Section 3.1c. Every component of this proposal is an extension of the four-year effort to have a village of sustainable community schools. . . . The collaborative nature of both the development of this proposal and the vision of our school culture, as well as how we frame Dyett's relationship to the community, also respond to these concerns. That Bronzeville parents want their children to assume their place as actors on local, national, and international stages and contribute to bettering their society and planet is specifically addressed in the Dyett mission. And the voiced need by parents and community members that young people know who they are, love their community and themselves, and are deeply rooted in their histories and cultures is also reflected in the mission and vision.[21]

Representatives also described how Dyett would have a restorative justice program, a full-time nurse, and a small student-to-counselor ratio to provide student support, beginning with a social-emotional assessment in the students' first year.[22]

After the presentations, the CPS representative thanked the three presenting groups for the "time, and the thoughtfulness, and the creativity and the ideas" behind each option to reopen Dyett before transitioning into the public comment period. "We're really excited to hear feedback from the community . . . that I will then share with the Board members." She went on to note that decorum was expected during the comment period: "I'm gonna ask the audience to remember that this is a fun and engaging event. Let's engage each other with dignity and respect." Last, she made another reference to opportunities to participate and share opinions beyond the meeting itself. "If you don't get to speak tonight, you have a phone number and email," she said, as well as exit slips that would be collected by meeting organizers. "There are many different ways in which your feedback can be shared with the board of education." This was a bizarre way to end the presentations. What was "fun and engaging" about the event, which was serious and even contentious? What would happen to the exit slips and any other feedback that was offered? How would it be used to make a decision?

As she finished speaking, audience members were already lining up behind the microphones on each side of the auditorium.

Attendees took the microphone for the next ninety minutes. Many, particularly those supporting the Coalition plan, read prepared statements. Supporters of the Coalition focused on the community's involvement with the development of their plan over many years, showing that the current proposal represented feedback and input from all the stakeholders. One woman quoted former mayor Harold Washington to make this point, saying that the Coalition had brought together "parents, students, teachers, community groups and partners, and university experts. The perfect formula for how to reimagine a school," much the same way Washington's campaign famously brought together Chicagoans from diverse backgrounds. Another commended the "thoughtful, diligent process" through which the plan was created. "This process was driven by parents and young people in partnership with scholars and academic experts to deliver a plan that has a solid academic focus."[23]

Several people supporting the Coalition's plan spoke about the role that history and the legacy of Bronzeville should play in the decision and argued that racism was the reason there was an RFP (request for proposals) procedure rather than an immediate response to a community-developed plan. "Walter H. Dyett is a historic institution that was founded as an open-enrollment Chicago Public School," said one speaker. "We want Captain Walter Henri Dyett honored by keeping it a Chicago Public School. We want you to respect our history and Bronzeville and the legacy of Walter H. Dyett." Seen this way, the "failing" school label itself failed by not encompassing a crucial detail about Dyett High School: that its very existence was a testimony to the history of black education in Bronzeville, to a hero and the geniuses under his care, to an institution that successfully educated black children to be great in an era when the expectations for their lives were meager. With this understanding, an attack on the legendary Dyett name was an attack on history and identity.

Another parent said forcefully, "At the end of the day, what we've got to stop doing is playing black and brown children. 'Cause that's what this is, a game. Dyett Global Leadership and Green Technology has to happen for our kids. 'Cause first of all, what we're *not* talking about is, CPS never would have reversed the decision if it wasn't for the community." This, of course, was a key fact that seemed lost and unacknowledged in the structure of the event. It's not as though CPS had come up with this proposals process of its own accord; it was the Coalition that had pushed the city to pull back from Brizard's depiction of a hollow, hopeless building marked by irredeemable failure. Dyett supporters had sacrificed time, safety, and energy to make this moment of reconsideration possible. Rather than considering their proposal on its own, CPS had established the RFP procedure and asked for these presentations, a move constituting a small but significant historical erasure. By contending that the RFP and the three proposals under consideration were operating in a market-based vacuum where they would compete and the best option would win, district officials were acting as though the city hall sit-ins, the demands on the alderman, and the civil rights complaint had never happened.[24]

"This is a sham," said one woman. "And this is disrespectful. This whole process has been disrespectful." When the meeting was nearly over, facilitators called Jitu Brown of the Kenwood-Oakland Community Organization (KOCO) up to speak but then, realizing he was one of the presenters, told him he was not eligible to make additional comments. This caused a massive uproar from the audience, leading the CPS facilitator to seize the microphone and try to explain. "So, we did not allow any of the presenters to sign up . . ." When people began to yell that Brown had indeed signed in to speak, she hurriedly apologized and abruptly concluded the meeting (without, as listed on the agenda, providing dates for the hearing or next steps) as people continued to shout in protest.

"I'm sorry. Then that was my fault. I'm so sorry. Out of respect for the evening, we're concluding today's community meeting. You have a phone number, you have an email address. Please complete your exit slips on the way out. Thank you." Frustration continued to echo across the auditorium as she rushed away.

For the next several weeks I found myself frequently checking the CPS website and the news for some hint of what was next for Dyett. The most glaring question was where the public hearing would be held, and at what time. Whether it was on the South Side or downtown at the CPS central offices would make a big difference to any community residents or members of the proposal teams who wanted to attend, especially those with inflexible work schedules, child care needs, or lack of reliable transportation.

A few weeks later, representatives from the Coalition called for a rally back at Alderman Burns's office, in search of more details about the Dyett hearing. A date had been announced, but no location. Everyone crowded into the foyer of the alderman's office. He seemed not to be present, but the director of constituent services came out to talk to the group. One organizer spoke up first. "The alderman needs to make sure the community knows where that's gonna be taking place, and what time that's going to be taking place. For such a critical decision, this should not be a mystery. Nobody at CPS seems to know anything about this, and it's unacceptable. This is a phantom process."

"Well, I'll make sure I give him that message about the transparency you're requesting," the director replied politely. He said he'd check to see what the chief of staff knew about the hearing, and he told people to call back at the end of the day. "But this has been weeks now," another community member piped up. "This has been weeks now. And they're still saying the scheduler, the chief of staff—you guys have been here [in the office] every day."

"Understood," said the director.

"We also need to know who makes the decision about Dyett. Is it the alderman? Because CPS says it's the alderman, and the alderman says it's CPS. We need clarity on who makes the decision about what takes place at Dyett High School. Everyone's pointing the finger. This is not a clear and transparent process." The director nodded solemnly and repeated the promise to let everyone know by the end of the day.

Chicago's schools are governed not by the Chicago City Council, but by a school board appointed by the mayor. But while aldermen do not have direct decision-making powers over CPS, they have a great deal of political power and can influence school happenings in indirect ways. And Burns was exceptionally influential in this regard: the preceding May, the mayor had appointed him chair of the city council's education committee, which the local newspaper called a "big political plum" and a "reward" for supporting the mayor's education agenda and helping him win black voters.[25] He would go on to wield this power in significant ways, such as single-handedly blocking discussion of a charter school moratorium supported by forty-two of the fifty aldermen.[26] Back in 2014, before any RFP procedure was launched, the mayor and the chair of the board of education both said they were interested in the Coalition's plan but would move forward on it only if Burns was supportive.[27] Burns's official-unofficial role in Dyett's future was confusing, and this confusion made the situation even more frustrating. When you can't get basic answers about how a supposedly democratic process is going to take place, it feels like a restriction of your ability to act as a citizen. As constituents in a system that seems constantly poised to wriggle out of our grasp, how much power can we ever really have?

The Coalition is hosting a big public barbecue to maintain momentum, morale, and support for its proposal. The event is also meant to celebrate the graduation of the school's last senior class. When the closure of Dyett was first announced and classes were phased out year by year, many of the school's resources and budgetary allocations dissolved as well. The students who remained in the shrinking school faced so many cuts that they were left to take courses in art, Spanish, social studies, and even physical education online.[28] Community members rallied to restore some rites of passage for the final thirteen seniors, such as luncheon and prom, and at this barbecue they will be honored for the achievement of completing high school. These efforts represent a "revitalization" that isn't contingent on the district or the decisions of faraway people; faced with the language of failure, it's a way of bringing resources and an eye toward the future to those students who have remained, rather than abandoning them.

When I get to the Dyett barbecue in Washington Park, I see a huge black and neon pink sign that says "SAVE DYETT" stuck in the ground. It's cloudy, but the intermittent raindrops go unnoticed by the folks lounging in chairs and bobbing their heads to the music as Dyett looms in the background, windows dark. Kids chase each other, toss a football back and forth, and play with hula hoops. The DJ is attending to the multiple generations of Chicago music fans present, playing mostly house music and occasional hip-hop.

After everyone has been eating and chatting for a while, the DJ turns down the music so the graduating Dyett seniors can be presented with gift baskets—literal laundry baskets filled with supplies and dormitory essentials. One of them takes the microphone to say thank you on behalf of the group. "I just wanna thank the community for being in this fight with us, so we can get our school," he says. Notably, even though he has already graduated from the old Dyett, when he says "our school" he's referring to the potential school of the future, the Dyett Global Leadership and Green Technology High School. Jitu Brown then takes the microphone. "We're in the fourth quarter of this fight," he says, praising and thanking everyone present who contributed to the Coalition's proposal. "We're giving the mayor a gift by showing a model for community engagement with schools." Brown then turns to address the seniors in a call-and-response.

"In your last year at Dyett, how did you take art class?"

"Online!"

He turns to the crowd. "Is that bad teachers?"

"No!" the group roars back.

"Is that bad parents?"

"No!"

"Is that bad students?"

"No!"

Another community member stands up to speak. "They don't think low-income African American families will be here in five years," she proclaims. "That's what this is about. . . . If Burns wants to get to Congress, he'll treat us with justice and respect," she adds, suggesting that Alderman Burns has long-run political aspirations beyond his aldermanic office that will require community support. Someone else suggests Burns has his eye on the mayor's office.

"No, he wants to be congressman!"

"Well, he shouldn't be dogcatcher," comes the response, spurring laughter. Conversation turns to next steps, and to the continued wait for information about the hearing. There's still no location or time, even though CPS has announced a date two weeks away. The *Hyde Park Herald*, a local neighborhood paper, has reported that the meeting will be downtown at CPS, but it didn't give a time, and it's unclear whether even the location is confirmed. While these details may seem minor since the hearing date is final, time and location have a big effect on who can attend and share their opinions. The meeting is scheduled for a Monday, making it difficult for people who work on weekdays to attend except in the evening. Chicago is also much more spread out geographically than many other cities, public transit is costly, and traveling from some parts of Bronzeville can be time consuming. The organizations behind each of the proposals could potentially rally resources for a bus to take people to CPS, but this would require coordination that becomes harder with each day that elapses without a clear time or location.

As days pass, it's like being caught in a time warp, where the days move more slowly than they should. There's no word from CPS about the next meeting, about a decision on Dyett, or about anything that would illuminate what happens next. The Coalition, undaunted, still engages the public to rally support for the school. I continue to wait for a time and location to be announced, staring at my calendar as though details might appear through sheer willpower. Everyone continues to wait. Over lunch at Peach's Restaurant, one of the former Dyett seniors tells me he doesn't think the hearing will happen at all. "Why haven't they told us where it is yet?" he asks pointedly, stirring a bowl of cheese grits. I'm beginning to wonder the same thing. Three days after the barbecue, several members of KOCO stage another sit-in at city hall, holding up signs, chanting, and blocking the elevators. When Will Burns appears to report to the city council chambers, he has to step over people to get to his office, and he's followed by jeers as he hurries away, speaking to no one. I wonder in that moment what he's thinking. What's it like to have the people you're supposed to represent shouting derisively at you? Didn't he become an elected official to serve the community? Now that the community is on his doorstep, making demands in righteous anger, does it give him pause or make him wonder if he's doing the right thing? How can he just keep walking? A teenage boy next to me, in city hall for some other business, watches incredulously as the police approach protesters. "They gonna go to jail for this?" he asks aloud of no one in particular.

Another day, Coalition members stand on the corner of 53rd and Lake Park hoisting the SAVE DYETT banner, and passing drivers honk in support: a Vienna Beef truck, a white moving van, a limousine. This last driver waves out the window, asking for an informational flyer. After a while I walk a couple of blocks down 53rd and get some cold bottled water from the dollar store. Everyone's melting in the sun, especially the older folks. *Too damn hot outside,* I write in my notebook. I wonder how much longer this is going to last, how many more arrests and hot days spent standing in the sun there will be. It's August 5. The hearing is supposed to happen on August 10, a Monday, and still no one has heard any details.

Sometime on Friday, August 7, this press release appears on the CPS website:

> Chicago Public Schools today announced the request for proposal process to identify a new open enrollment, neighborhood high school at the current site of Dyett High School is being extended to provide adequate time to review community feedback and proposals.
>
> CPS is also moving the public hearing on the proposals to 6 p.m. on September 15, 2015 inside the Board of Education Chambers at 42 West Madison.
>
> "Chicago Public Schools is committed to a community driven process that will identify a high-quality education option for the former Dyett site," said Forrest Claypool, CEO of CPS. "We continue to review the applications by the 2014 RFP, but with the budget and financial crisis dominating the focus of the new CPS administration, more time is necessary to make an informed recommendation to the Board of Education. We look forward to receiving further feedback at the upcoming community hearing."[29]

Another CEO. Claypool replaced Byrd-Bennett after the federal investigation involving her was announced. Another CEO, another procedural delay, another set of mysteries. Why was more time needed to review just three proposals? And given that a decision at the August 10 hearing was never promised, why postpone the meeting a month? Was there a commitment that the board would make a decision at the September 15 hearing, or would a final decision be postponed again? Further, Claypool's words about a "community-driven process" were strange given that community efforts seemed to be consistently met with district resistance or delay. Sure, the community was driving the process, but it seemed that only CPS could determine the destination.

> You have to more than want to do it—you have to will yourself to do it.
>
> —Walter H. Dyett[30]

> The last straw was when CPS violated its own rules. Two proposals were submitted on time, but then CPS accepted a late proposal. . . . When CPS cancelled the August 10 public hearing—the last planned hearing on the proposals before a scheduled August 26 School Board vote [subsequently moved to September]—with no notice, we drew the line in the sand and said no more. . . . I never wanted to be in front of a camera. All I wanted was to be part of my kids' education and be part of the solution. I just wanted to drop my children off and know that they would be educated the way I was. But I found every day that that was far from the reality. I now want children in this city and country to know that there are people out there fighting, willing to go hungry—for them.
>
> —Jeanette Taylor-Ramann[31]

The Coalition formally announced the hunger strike while standing in the broad green space in front of Dyett. News cameras and reporters gathered around as Jitu Brown began to speak. Today several members of the Coalition, along with activists and community allies, were beginning a monumental undertaking. They vowed not to eat until the mayor agreed to move forward with the Dyett Global Leadership and Green Technology High School.[32]

> We're gonna need your spirit and your energy, because we don't know how long we're gonna need to be out here. . . . This is a referendum on where we live. It's a referendum on the people in power. But one thing we've learned as organizers is, it's not about how eloquent we are. It's not who the people are that you know on the inside. What it's about is, do you have the will to win? . . . We don't care that it's a new board. We don't care that it's a new CEO. That's their problem. What CPS has earned is our mistrust. We know that they will lie. We know that they will play the shell game. They've done it. How many meetings have we been in with temporary people in CPS who talk like they're with us and then they stab the community in the back? We're done with that. We were supposed to have a hearing on August 10, and a board vote on August 26, and we want this school. And we want this school as the hub of a sustainable community school village. We want [local elementary schools like] Mollison. We want Till. We want Fiske. We want Fuller. We want them all. And that's what time it is. We don't trust them with our children. We don't trust them. This is not rhetoric. . . . They killed this school. And so we have no more patience for this.

Brown also referred specifically to one justification in the press release for why the hearing was delayed—that new board members had just been appointed. Chicago does not have an elected school board like every other district and municipality in the state of Illinois; instead, the mayor appoints the school board. Emanuel had just appointed four new board members. He also appointed his chief of staff, Forrest Claypool, to replace Byrd-Bennett as CEO. The argument from the district was that these new decision makers needed more time to review the proposals.

There was reason to believe the hunger strike could be effective: direct historical precedent. In 2001, fourteen parents and community members in Little Village, a Mexican American neighborhood north and west of Dyett, held a nineteen-day hunger strike after CPS promised a new building to relieve overcrowding in the neighborhood school, then delayed the project. The strikers camped out in tents on the land sited for the school, which they called Camp Cesar Chavez. Paul Vallas, CEO at the time, refused to meet with them or negotiate or respond to what he called blackmail. "I'm not going to locate it on a site because people are threatening not to eat. You could have one of these [protests] a week," he said. When Vallas left Chicago and was replaced as CEO by Arne Duncan, Duncan declared that he had "a hell of a lot of respect for [the protesters]" and agreed to move forward with the new school.

Could the same story unfold in Bronzeville? *This is a referendum on where we live*. Conceding to the board, stepping back and letting them renege on their word or reroute the process they had already established, or create a whole new process, would be like conceding that their version of the world—their vision from beyond the Veil—had merit. In their world Dyett was a failure. Nothing worth saving. A disposable school serving disposable people, to be moved around in whatever ways were convenient at the moment. This moment was a referendum on the history, legacy, and future of Bronzeville and on the right to black educational self-determination.

"ALL OF US WANTED DYETT"

Like many other aspects of CPS's bureaucratic functioning, attending a board of education meeting is theoretically very easy and practically not easy at all. Meetings are open to the public, but they always take place at 10:30 on Wednesday morning—an awkward time for working parents or teachers. You have to sign up in advance, and the online registration notoriously fills up and closes within minutes of opening. Many days before the August 26 meeting, I had set my alarm early so I could get my name on the register the second it opened. I thought back to several weeks before, when this meeting was supposed to be the day the board would make a final determination on Dyett. Now things seemed no closer to a resolution. When I arrived at the meeting the chambers were already full, and I had to sit in an overflow room watching the proceedings on closed-circuit television. When it was time for public comment, Bronzeville resident and hunger striker Jeanette Taylor-Ramann took the podium and spoke, despite appearing tired and physically weak. She was wrapped in a blanket. "The only mistake I ever made was being born black," she said to the board.

Others took the podium, talking about other issues unrelated to Dyett, and each speaker shed light on another way the city was struggling. The board proceedings mandate extremely strict time limits, with a large red digital countdown clock, and as people stepped to the microphone asking for care and attention toward things extremely important to them, each was met by dispassionate stares from the people on the dais. It was a depressing display, like some feudal society, with subjects asking for mercy from a panel of powerful lords. A mother told the board how her homeless children were denied the transportation benefits they were supposed to receive from the district and she had to spend food money to get them to school on public transit. The treasurer of the Chicago Teachers Union spoke of how proposed special education cuts would hurt students with disabilities; when she began to cry, she was removed by security. A teenage girl said that her college and career counselor was being laid off and she didn't know how she would get to college; she was also removed by security.

Suddenly a member of the Coalition burst into the overflow room. "Is anyone here a doctor? Jeanette just fainted." Everyone looked up at him wide-eyed, and he whirled away. I got up and went to the exit, where a security guard stood. "Yes? There's no room in the chambers," the guard said, moving between me and the door. I peered around him, craning my neck to see Jeanette Taylor-Ramann being carried out on a stretcher. The meeting continued uninterrupted.

Eight days later, CPS announced that Dyett would be reopened.

At the press conference, Will Burns stood on the podium, raising a finger to emphasize his points as he spoke. "We *all* fought for Dyett. Together," he said, with CEO Claypool standing behind him. "All of us wanted Dyett to be an open enrollment public high school."[33] I thought about how this would look to the broader public—this black elected official proclaiming his unflinching support. I thought back to the day I watched Burns step over the bodies of protestors across the floor of city hall, and I wondered which *we* he was referring to.

Dyett was to become an open-enrollment arts high school, featuring an "innovation technology lab." Despite the talk about "innovation," the Coalition's plan would not be used and was not acknowledged or referred to in any way in the press release. In fact, none of the proposals or any aspect of the RFP was mentioned in the press release.[34] It was as if it had never happened.

"They have won," said Congressman Bobby Rush, speaking of the hunger strikers. No Coalition members were in the room to hear him, however. They were not admitted to the chambers where the press conference took place. They sat outside.

The next day Jitu Brown told Amy Goodman of *Democracy Now!* that the hunger strike would continue:

> We do not see this as a victory. This is not a victory for the children in Bronzeville. . . . I got a call from CPS CEO Forrest Claypool 15 minutes before the press conference, that we were locked out of by CPS, and he told me—I asked him, "Well, where is the room for negotiation?" And he said, "Well, we're moving forward." So my message to him today is: So are we. We're moving forward. . . . This is not something that we take lightly. These are our children. These are our communities. We have to live with CPS reforms after the people that implement them get promoted to some other job. So we will determine the type of education that our children receive in Bronzeville."[35]

Why do people fight for schools like Dyett? Why did the Coalition continue to fight even after those in power assured them of their own victory? Because it was never just about Dyett. A fight for a school is never just about a school. A school means the potential for stability in an unstable world, the potential for agency in the face of powerlessness, the enactment of one's own dreams and visions for one's own children. Because whether you're in Detroit or Austin or Louisiana or Chicago, you want to feel that your school is *your* school. That you have some say in the matter, that your voice can make a difference. You want to feel that the rules are fair, not that you're playing a shell game. You want to feel like a citizen. So you fight.

Two weeks later the hunger strike is still on. I ride the bus to attend a candlelight vigil in support. We meet at Operation PUSH, then together we begin a silent march. It's a short walk—south on Drexel to 51st Street. If we took a right we would hit Washington

Park, and it's a short walk to Dyett. But we take a left. To the president's house.

I've always thought it fascinating that President Barack Obama's house is so close to Dyett. It's a little over a half mile away, less than fifteen minutes on foot. In the summer I'd pass it on the way from my apartment to the school. As we stand outside now, the house obscured by the trees, I wonder what kind of community organizer the president was in his time. I wonder if, since becoming secretary of education, Arne Duncan has ever told him the story of the Little Village hunger strike, and whether he would, like Duncan, have a "hell of a lot of respect" for his neighbors, who have now gone twenty-five days without food in order to see their vision enacted for a school his own daughters could attend if they wanted. I think about how each of these men had the freedom to choose his own children's education, and how each chose the private University of Chicago Laboratory Schools, where Rahm Emanuel's children are also enrolled. I wonder why it always feels as if some Chicagoans have to fight for everything and others don't.

Nine days later, the hunger strike was over.

WHAT A SCHOOL MEANS

> I hated to end the strike, because I didn't want the mayor or the aldermen to feel like we were giving up. But we had to end it because we knew that the mayor would leave us out there to die.
>
> —Anna Jones, hunger striker[36]

The Dyett hunger strike ended on September 20, 2015, after thirty-four days and two hospitalizations. At a press conference, hunger striker Monique Redeaux-Smith addressed the crowd:

> While we cannot yet claim complete victory, we do understand that our efforts so far have been victorious in a number of ways. . . . Through community resistance, [Dyett] was slated to be reopened in 2016–17. And even though there was a request for proposals, we know that the plan for that space *was* to become another privatized school within Bronzeville. But again, with community resistance and this hunger strike, we pushed CPS and the Mayor to commit to reopening Dyett as a public, open-enrollment neighborhood school. And that is a victory.[37]

The members of the Coalition did not see their plan for Dyett come to fruition. But they garnered national attention for a struggle that, years earlier, had implicitly been declared dead. "There are some schools so far gone that you cannot save them," Brizard had said, declaring that the building was devoid of hope. Those who fought for Dyett understood that what was on paper a question of numbers actually reflected the belief that their lives, their children's lives, and their hopes did not matter. The end came only when it became apparent how deep that disregard really was, and the fight became a matter of life or death in a terrifyingly immediate way.

Derrick Bell, a renowned legal scholar whose work is considered seminal in the construction of critical race theory, wrote about the concept of *interest convergence*: the idea that black people will be permitted to achieve a measure of racial equality only in moments and through methods that happen to serve the interests of white people—that is, when the interests of black people and those of white people converge.[38] In a sense the final Dyett decision is an example of interest convergence. The school was able to reopen, but only at a time and in a fashion that served the mayor's political interests and did not set a precedent for the meaningful inclusion of community voices in deciding school policy—a precedent that would not have converged with white interests in the schools or in the city writ large.

Today the lights are back on at the huge black building in Washington Park. Walter H. Dyett High School for the Arts boasts almost $15 million in new investments, including facilities for dance, textile design, and music.[39] And starting in sophomore year all students are required to take music. When the school opened for its first (new) day in 2016, the building greeted a new freshman class of 150 students, above the target of 125. And 85 percent of them were from the area immediately surrounding the school. When asked what she thought of the new Dyett, one of the new students said, “We value our education more because of what people sacrificed.”[40]

I have looked through a lot of old photographs of Walter Henri Dyett. Dyett served in the military, and I have seen his portraits in uniform. I have seen photos of him in childhood. I have seen photographs of him leading distinguished musicians arrayed in perfect rows, in pristine black-and-white formal wear. I have seen him at the front of his classroom, orchestrating music from the students known as “the Captain’s kids,” some of whom lied about their addresses to study under him.[41] But my favorite photograph shows Dyett standing in Washington Park (fig. 3). It’s spring, and several young women are gathered for a baton-twirling training camp, learning to be majorettes. My own grandmother, who was born in Mississippi and migrated north in 1943, was a baton twirler, and I always envied the skill. In the photo, Dyett stands amid the trees and seems unaware of the camera. He’s demonstrating how to twirl the baton as the girls watch intently. The girls wear shorts, and Dyett’s sleeves are rolled up. When I look at the photo I think of these regular days as an educator, the mo-

FIGURE 3 Dyett leading Du Sable High School spring baton-twirling camp (likely in Washington Park), June 1940. Source: Walter Henri Dyett Papers, box 7, folder 70, Vivian G. Harsh Research Collection of Afro-American History and Literature, Chicago Public Library.

ments that don't make headlines but that make all the hard work feel worth it. The moments of intense focus and commitment where trying to help someone understand seems like the most important thing in the world, deserving all your energy. In this photo I see Dyett not as a historical luminary, the person whose name ends up over the door of a building, but as an ordinary person trying to do what he can for the young people of Bronzeville. I see a warm day in Washington Park, with people convened to be together but also to pursue something they think is vital for their lives.

And this, in the end, is what the fight for Dyett was about. It was about honoring the everyday moments that make a school a place of care, a home, a site of history. It was about saying *this is not a failed school, and we are not failed people. We know our history. We will prevail. You will not kill us.*

The city of Chicago still has black people, and it still has black schools. But, as we will see in the next chapter, it's certainly not for lack of trying.

2 *City of Losses*

We are things of dry hours and the involuntary plan,
Grayed in, and gray. . . .
—Gwendolyn Brooks, "kitchenette building"

The kitchenette is the funnel through which our pulverized
lives flow to ruin and death on the city pavements, at a profit.
—Richard Wright, *12 Million Black Voices*

WHAT IT IS, AND WHAT IT IS NOT

The wood-paneled room was packed with parents, students, and teachers. A smattering of applause stirred the crowd as the regional science fair winners returned to their seats, guided gently by teachers. The president of the Chicago Board of Education watched the scene from the wooden dais, seated beneath an oversized painted seal of the city of Chicago. "We will now proceed with the business portion of the meeting," he said, looking down at a piece of paper while holding the microphone gingerly with his left hand. "And, uh, with the CEO's report. Barbara?"

Barbara Byrd-Bennett stood at the lectern, reading glasses balanced low on her nose. As CPS CEO, she was tasked with overseeing hundreds of schools and thousands of students in the nation's third-largest public school system. Appointed almost one year earlier by the city's mayor, Rahm Emanuel, she now faced a crucial moment in her tenure as a leader: explaining, at a monthly board meeting open to the press and the public and recorded on video, why the district was planning to close fifty-four schools at the end of the academic year.

Community members had for months been loudly registering their ire at the potential closings, reacting first to a much longer list of 129 schools facing possible closure. Many educators and activists were especially incensed by the racial breakdown of the proposed closures: 80 percent of the students who would be affected were African American (about twice the proportion of black students in the district), and 87 percent of the schools to be closed were majority black.[1] In an open letter denouncing the plan, one pastor called it a misguided attempt at "'playing God' by uprooting and mass shifting poor children and disrupting their fragile communities"; he referred to it as "massive planned chaos . . . the contemporary version of separate and unequal public education policy."[2] Chicago Teachers Union President Karen Lewis held a press conference in front of Mahalia Jackson Elementary School on the city's South Side, calling the planned closures "outrageous" and explicitly racist: "There is no way people of conscience will stand by and allow these people to shut down nearly a third of our school district without putting up a fight," she told gathered supporters. "Most of these campuses are in the Black community. . . . And this is by design."[3] One activist, Valerie Leonard, was quoted in the press as remarking, "[Mayor Rahm Emanuel] wants to turn around the city of Chicago, make a new Chicago. Does that new Chicago mean no black folks?"[4] While these allegations would be stinging in any context, they carried special weight in Chicago, a city as famous for its deep-rooted segregation as for its sports teams and bad weather.

Now it was Byrd-Bennett's turn to answer her critics and explain her stance that the school closings were the right choice for the city. It was up to her to respond to the sentiments of people like Leonard and to the suggestion that school closings not only were racist in themselves, but were part of a historical pattern and a larger plan to push black residents out of Chicago by making the city functionally uninhabitable. How can parents live in a neighborhood with no schools? As reporters, parents, and teachers clustered in the small board chamber, she began to read a prepared statement. At first she avoided any mention of race, making only an oblique reference to segregation by mentioning students in "certain parts" of the city.

> For too long, children in certain parts of our city have been cheated out of the resources they need to succeed in the classroom because they are trapped in underutilized schools. These underutilized schools are also under-resourced. Today, Chicago has 145,000 fewer school-aged children than it did in the year 2000. This has affected student enrollment, especially on the city's South and West sides, which saw significant population declines and now have the most underutilized schools.[5]

But as she continued, Byrd-Bennett began to address the allegations of racism more directly. "What I *cannot* understand, and *will* not accept, is that the proposals I am offering are racist." As she spoke, slowly and deliberately, someone in the crowd shouted angrily, "They are!" Byrd-Bennett paused, waiting for quiet. For a moment she looked less like a city official than like the veteran Harlem principal she was—a disciplinarian waiting for her students to settle down before proceeding. She repeated the line slightly louder, sternly and with conviction.

> What I *cannot* understand, and *will* not accept, is that the proposals I am offering are racist. That is an affront to me as a woman of color. And it is an affront to every parent in our community who demands a better education for their children. First, the overwhelming majority of students in CPS are children of color. Any significant change in the status quo, therefore, is going to affect those children. This is not racist, it's simply a fact. Second, the greatest population losses in our city over the past decade have taken place in the South and the West sides. Underutilized schools in these areas are the result of demographic changes and not race.

Recounting her own background growing up in predominantly African American schools, Byrd-Bennett added, "Believe me—I know what racism is, and what racism is not.

What racism is, and what racism is not. Byrd-Bennett's forceful statement makes it all sound cut-and-dried. But can it really be so simple? If thousands of black children are displaced by school closings, what does it mean to refer to the disproportionate impact they bear as "not racist, simply a fact"? Byrd-Bennett calls the schools underresourced and underutilized, suggesting that some outside actor is responsible for underresourcing and underutilizing them. Since Byrd-Bennett is head of the district, we might assume that she herself is responsible for how the schools are resourced or utilized. But the responsible actor remains invisible, unnamed and therefore not culpable. Thus, in the end, a speech intended to give a straightforward explanation—*Why are the schools being closed? Because they are underutilized*—instead provokes a series of further questions about the history that led us to this moment. What happened to drive down enrollment in these schools? And how does knowing this history help us understand why people were so vociferously opposed to the school closings?

The story of the underresourced and underutilized schools—and how they got that way—began long before Byrd-Bennett came to Chicago. In fact, it began long before she was born. In this chapter I will try to fill in the blanks in her statement by traveling a century back in time, because is not possible to fundamentally understand the 2013 school closings in Bronzeville without knowing the history of the community. By studying how social systems have arisen over time, we can see not only how things are now, but how they could be otherwise. The present is not inevitable; things have come to be as we know them through human actors. If we understand the genesis of our present, we have a chance of changing the future.

WELCOME TO THE BLACK METROPOLIS

Sometimes this connection between the past, the present, and the future feels perfectly obvious. Standing on the corner of 47th and King Drive, I feel I can look back in time almost as easily as I look down the street. If I turn my attention from the cars rushing by and the rumble of the Green Line elevated train, symbols of this intersection's past are everywhere. On the four corners stand four tall pillars, and topping each is a bronze statue of a jazz musician—one is on sax, one plays a long-necked bass guitar, one is on clarinet, and the fourth is the bandleader, keeping time with his hand raised triumphantly. A man in a suit, carrying the *Chicago Defender* under his arm, slows his stride to check his reflection in the window of Peach's Restaurant and adjust his collar.

On the southwest corner is a vacant lot where someone has built raised garden beds and painted wooden pillars with the sun, plants, and inspirational messages and faces from black history. Adjacent to the lot is a three-story graystone with an enclosed stone balcony; once stately, it's now boarded up. On the southeast corner is the Harold Washington Cultural Center, where the inscription on a statue of Chicago's first black mayor reminds us that he was a "consummate statesman, a political genius." On the northeast corner sits H-Dogs, a burger and hot dog restaurant owned by chef Cliff Rome. Rome also owns Peach's, as well as a catering business, an art gallery, and the historic Parkway Ballroom.

Pedestrian traffic is light but steady, and cars speed along the wide, heavily landscaped boulevard. When the 47th Street bus pulls up at the same time as the King Drive express, a chorus of honks, whistles, and calls erupts as people tell the bus driver to wait for a woman in scrubs rushing across the street to catch her transfer. A man pulls over near me and rolls down his car window. He asks if there's a Jewel grocery store farther east on 47th. I tell him there isn't but that he can go up to the one on 35th. "I hate that one!" he exclaims before driving away. Everyone else I encounter—a man in a workman's blue uniform, a woman in a pink skirt waiting to cross the street, three men sitting on the median watching traffic go by—greets me with a smile, "how you doin'," or "hey, pretty girl."

I'm hungry, so I step into Peach's, open daily from 7:00 to 3:00, serving breakfast and lunch. A sign outside shows an illustration of a young girl with soft eyes, hair in pigtails, looking over her shoulder. Inside, I recognize the hostess—she's my brother's close friend and neighbor, and her son often plays with my niece. A large chalkboard wall displays the specials, and I know right away that I want chicken wings and French toast. I chat with my waitress about the special menu Peach's served on Father's Day (ribs and gumbo).

As I eat, I open a thick, heavy book—*Black Metropolis: A Study of Negro Life in a Northern City*. It's a reminder that I'm not the first sociologist to document my time at this very intersection.

In their classic volume from 1945, St. Clair Drake and Horace Cayton describe the corner. One of the street signs has changed—King Drive was South Park Way before it was renamed in 1968—like so many black urban thoroughfares—after the assassination of Dr. Martin Luther King Jr. But other than that, Drake and Cayton's narrative sounds awfully familiar.

> Stand in the center of the Black Belt—at Chicago's 47th St. and South Parkway.[6] Around you swirls a continuous eddy of faces—black, brown, olive, yellow, and white. Soon you will realize that this is not "just another neighborhood" of the Midwest Metropolis. Glance at the newsstand at the corner. . . . [Y]ou will also find a number of weeklies headlining the activities of Negroes—Chicago's *Defender*, *Bee*, *News-Ledger*, and *Metropolitan News*, the Pittsburgh *Courier*, and a number of others. In the nearby drugstore colored clerks are bustling about. . . . Two large theaters will catch your eye with their billboards featuring Negro orchestras and vaudeville troupes. . . . On a spring or summer day this spot, "47th and South Park," is the urban equivalent of a village square. In fact, Black Metropolis has a saying, "If you're trying to find a certain Negro in Chicago, stand on the corner of 47th and South Park long enough and you're bound to see him." There is continuous and colorful movement here.[7]

Given the seventy-year difference in our observations, it's striking how closely Drake and Cayton's description mirrors my own—businesses owned and staffed by black people, the familiar faces, the *Defender*. But in other ways our descriptions differ. How did the beautiful graystone residence come to be vacant and boarded up? Although cars pass playing songs by Rihanna and Future, why is it that these artists aren't likely to perform at music venues in the community the way Lena Horne and Louis

Armstrong once did—memorialized by the bronze musicians towering over the street? How did the hum of black social life—the friendly faces, the "how are you" greetings—dwindle from the "continuous eddy" that Drake and Cayton describe? The answer has something to do with the population loss Byrd-Bennett described, but it goes much deeper than she let on. To understand what the corner of 47th and King Drive looks like today, we have to begin our story much earlier.

BECOMING BRONZEVILLE

For the first decades of its existence the city of Chicago had few black residents. In 1900 the city was home to about 30,000 black people—about 1.8 percent of the total population.[8] Facing segregation, excluded and ignored by the city's business community, these residents congregated in one area, as did most other citizens of Chicago, a city of neighborhoods and ethnic enclaves.

The other ethnic groups who arrived in Chicago at the beginning of the twentieth century (including Poles, Germans, Italians, and Scandinavians) followed the pattern familiar to immigrants across the country: as generations established themselves in the United States and learned English, they "steadily moved away from these areas of first settlement into more desirable areas of second settlement" before assimilating into the general population.[9] But black Chicagoans were different. During the first Great Migration, as World War I drove hundreds of thousands of African Americans northward in search of industrial employment (and in flight from the social and political persecution of the South), Chicago's black population swelled to about 109,000 in 1920: 3.6 times what it was two decades earlier, a growth rate more than twice that of the city overall. Labor recruiters traveled by train throughout the South, urging black people to move north. Drake and Cayton describe the recruiters' techniques: "They sometimes carried free tickets in their pockets, and always glowing promises on their tongues. . . . And as each wave [of laborers] arrived, the migrants wrote the folks back home about the wonderful North. A flood of relatives and friends followed in their wake," and the weekly Negro newspaper the *Defender* published open letters imploring migrants to join their kin in the big city and turn their backs on the South: "Have they stopped their Jim Crow cars? Can you buy a Pullman sleeper where you wish? . . . [T]o their section of the country we have said, as the song goes, 'I hear you calling me,' and have boarded the train singing 'Good-bye, Dixie Land.' "[10]

Notably, these residents did not disperse across the city like their European counterparts—they stayed in one place. While the same cultural homophily that united ethnic enclaves in other parts of the city doubtless played a role, African Americans also feared racial violence. From 1917 to 1921, fifty-eight bombs struck the homes of black residents, of bankers who gave them mortgages, or of real estate agents who sold them property. As the Chicago Commission on Race Relations noted,[11] these bombings caused two deaths and did $100,000 of damage, averaging one bombing every twenty days over three years and eight months. These bombings were part of "a general scheme to close the channels through which the invasion [of black people] proceeded."[12]

One repeated target of the bombings was Jesse Binga. Binga was born in Detroit, the son of a barber. In his twenties he moved to Chicago, where he held a variety of jobs before settling on entrepreneurial real estate. In 1908 he became head of the city's first black-owned financial institution when he founded the Binga Bank. In this role he was able to provide mortgages to black residents who had been denied home loans by other banks. He also bought a home at 59th and South Park, beyond the nascent boundaries of black Chicago. For these sins he paid a price, as the commission report describes:

> On November 12, 1919, an automobile rolled by [Binga's] realty office and a bomb was tossed from it. It left the office in ruins. . . . Twenty-one days later an automobile drew up in front of Binga's home at 5922 South Park Avenue, and its occupants put a bomb under the front steps. It failed to explode. When the firemen arrive they found it sizzling in the slush beneath the porch. The police declared that this was an expression of racial feeling. Twenty-five days later the bombers reappeared and left a third bomb. It tore up the porch of Binga's home. Again the police found that the explosion had been caused by "racial feeling," white men having said that "Binga rented too many flats to Negroes in high-class residence districts."[13]

After the third bombing, police were assigned to guard Binga's home in shifts; during a shift change on February 28, 1920, a police guard's late arrival left an opening and a fourth bomb was thrown at the house. It landed in a puddle. Binga's home was bombed a fifth time three months later, completely destroying the front of the house and shattering windows in surrounding houses. Despite Binga's offering a $1,000 reward to determine who was behind the bombings, a *sixth* explosion struck his property in November of that year, and no one was ever arrested for any of the attacks.

This campaign also included harassment in the media of real estate brokers of any race who helped black people buy in white areas; they were labeled "unclean outcasts of society to be boycotted and ostracized in every possible manner" because they had violated "a gentleman's obligation to his community in selling a home to a Negro."[14]

Current and potential black homeowners faced threatening phone calls and letters. Crede Hubbard, of 43rd and Vincennes, told the police he had received a phone call the day he was to move into his new house. A man calling himself "Mr. Day of the Hyde Park and Kenwood Association" told him, "We have spent a lot of money and we want to keep this district white." He pressured Hubbard to sell his property; when Hubbard refused, he received a visit a week later from another homeowners' association member; Mr. Austin told him, "You will understand that you are not welcome in this district. . . . Why do you persist in wanting to live here when you know you are not wanted?" As the man left the home he said, "You had better consider this proposition." Later a railroad clerk told Hubbard he had received a letter from Mr. Austin instructing him to "use whatever influence you have to induce him to sell and find out for us his lowest figures." The next week, during a trip to Milwaukee, Hubbard read in the newspaper that his home had been bombed while his children slept.

Similar patterns emerged in each of the fifty-eight bombings, and the conclusion of the investigating commission on the matter was damning: "In all these fifty-eight bombings the police have been able to accomplish nothing definite. Practically every incident involved an automobile, descriptions of which were furnished by witnesses. The precautions taken to prevent bombings, even if they were well planned and systematically carried out, failed lamentably."[15]

Given this context, where violence and intimidation were used to maintain the borders between Chicago's black residential corridor and the rest of the city, it is no surprise that African American residents remained bound together in one area. By the 1920s this region of Chicago between 22nd and 51st Streets was known as the "Black Belt," the "Black ghetto," or, worse, "Darkie Town." James J. Gentry, theater critic for the black newspaper the *Chicago Bee*, suggested to Anthony Overton, the paper's owner, that the *Bee* use the more pleasing term "Bronzeville." (It may or may not be a coincidence that Overton, who made his fortune selling cosmetics to the black community, would appreciate a term that referred artfully to his readers' skin tone.) When Gentry left the *Bee* in 1932 and pitched his idea for a "Mayor of Bronzeville" contest to Robert Sengstacke Abbott, publisher of the *Defender*, the name stuck.[16] When black children moved with their families from the South to Chicago, they found themselves in this tightly circumscribed environment. Although full of faces like their own, it was a small world, and the consequences for leaving its borders were dire.

THE INVISIBLE FENCE

In addition to physical violence, restrictive covenants—private agreements between property owners and real estate agents that homes were not be sold to or occupied by black people—made it extraordinarily difficult for African Americans to find housing in other parts of the city. One member of the Chicago Real Estate Board (CREB) called restrictive covenants "a marvelous delicately-woven chain armour . . . [excluding] any member of a race not Caucasian."[17] The CREB actively encouraged restrictive covenants, sending advocates and speakers across the city to praise the strategy to white property owners.[18] It also voted to expel any of its members who rented or sold to black people on a block otherwise occupied by white residents.[19] Besides directly preventing black people from finding homes in white areas, restrictive covenants served as informal signals to institutional gatekeepers. As legal scholar Richard R. W. Brooks has argued, even once restrictive covenants were legally unenforceable, "lawyers, lenders, realtors, insurers and government agencies continued to rely on covenants as proxies for the racial exclusivity and class of neighborhoods."[20] By the time they were outlawed in the 1948 Supreme Court ruling in *Shelley v. Kraemer*, restrictive covenants had served their purpose[21] by reinforcing a sort of invisible fence around Bronzeville. Ironically, even though this fence was created and forcibly maintained through fear, violence, and discrimination, it also set the stage for a degree of economic, political, and creative vitality for black Chicagoans.

As a consequence of its spatial isolation, Bronzeville became a semiautonomous residential and business district. Bronzeville residents also enjoyed some political autonomy; in 1928 they elected Congressman Oscar DePriest after a successful political career begun as the community's alderman, making him the North's first black member of the US House of Representatives.

The community also became a hub of black artistic and intellectual production. Jazz clubs peppered State Street beginning in the 1920s as King Oliver, Louis Armstrong, and Jelly Roll Morton brought their talents from the South.[22] Bronzeville was home to the *Chicago Defender* newspaper, which, through nationwide distribution, played a role in both articulating and shaping the political opinions of African Americans across the country. Cultural luminaries Ida B. Wells, Richard Wright, Gwendolyn Brooks, Sam Cooke, Nat King Cole, and Mahalia Jackson all called Bronzeville home at some point. Like other black people in so many spaces at so many times, Bronzeville residents responded to white supremacy by shaping their space in their own image, turning "humiliating and dehumanizing segregation into exhilarating and rehumanizing congregation."[23] Sociologist George Lipsitz refers to this resilient reframing as part of a *black spatial imaginary*, a way of understanding the physical world through the "socially shared understanding of the importance of public space as well as its power to create new opportunities and life chances."[24]

But the relative economic autonomy of Bronzeville also left the area especially vulnerable to the financial fortunes of its community members. As the 1920s came to a close, the Great Depression shattered the economic prospects of many black Chicagoans, while new white-owned business developments and chain stores along 47th Street began to entice shoppers who had previously kept their consumer dollars within the community.[25]

Furthermore, Bronzeville increasingly had another problem: housing. The first Great Migration slowed during the years of the Depression as work dried up, but it picked up again after World War II. Soon Bronzeville's swelling population, combined with the limitations of violence and restrictive covenants, inevitably produced a skyrocketing density that made life hard for residents. Property owners began dividing buildings into tiny "kitchenettes," single rooms with a hot plate instead of a real kitchen, where multiple family members might share the space and also share bathrooms with neighbors down the hall. For many Bronzeville children, this was what home looked like (fig. 4).

In his classic novel *Native Son*, renowned author Richard Wright brought the kitchenette to life through the eyes of his protagonist, Bigger Thomas, but he also described his own experience of living in one in *12 Million Black Voices*:

> What they do is this: they take, say, a seven-room apartment, which rents for $50 a month to whites, and cut it up into seven small apartments, of one room each; they install one small gas stove and one small sink in each room. The Bosses of the Buildings rent these kitchenettes to us at the rate of, say, $6 a week. Hence, the same apartment for which white people—who can

FIGURE 4 Children standing in front of a kitchenette building on South Park Way (now King Drive), formerly a well-to-do avenue. Source: Edwin Rosskam, photographer. US Farm Security Administration, 1941. Retrieved from the Library of Congress, https://www.loc.gov/item/fsa1997015740/PP.

> get jobs anywhere and who receive higher wages than we—pay $50 a month is rented to us for $42 a week! And because there are not enough houses for us to live in, because we have been used to sleeping several in a room on the plantations in the South, we rent these kitchenettes and are glad to get them. . . . The kitchenette is the author of the glad tidings that new suckers are in town, ready to be cheated, plundered, and put in their places. The kitchenette is our prison, our death sentence without a trial, the new form of mob violence that assaults not only the lone individual, but all of us, in its ceaseless attacks.[26]

By 1940 Bronzeville's population was over 150,000, squeezed into an area of about three square miles—twice the city's average density.[27] The community was like one big kitchenette—lots of people crammed into a very small space. Inevitably, two municipal institutions would have to confront the rising population in Bronzeville: the public school system and the public housing system.[28]

PHANTOMS ON STATE STREET: THE RISE AND FALL OF PUBLIC HOUSING IN BRONZEVILLE

> I remember very clearly the conditions at 41st and King: roach-infested, vermin-infested. I used to sit up nights and chase the mice away from my younger brothers. There were three of us, and it was a one-room kind of a situation, maybe two. It was a three-story building, which would have been a six-flat, and each of the flats was subdivided at least once. We had twelve families living in a structure that was designed to accommodate six. It was a lot of people and minimal privacy. And I remember moving into Ida B.—the new shiny stoves and refrigerators, and then a living room and a kitchen. It was nice and spacious clean and well-lit, and it was home! Ida B. Wells was a step up.
>
> —Bennie L. Crane, Ida B. Wells resident, 1943–54[29]

When the Ida B. Wells Homes officially opened in Bronzeville in 1941, its first residents had no way of anticipating that it would be the first of many such public housing developments that would come to define the landscape of the Bronzeville community so prominently or so notoriously—or that, by the time they were torn down, in the eyes of the public they would be a symbol of the worst kind of violence and urban decay. For children like Bennie L. Crane and their families, "Ida B." was simply home, and it was a marked improvement over kitchenette living.[30]

The Ida B. Wells Homes were built as part of an effort at "slum clearance" by the four-year-old Chicago Housing Authority, founded in response to the 1937 Housing Act that set out to reform America's poorest residential communities by providing federal support to locally established housing authorities. The project was built on the site of razed housing deemed substandard by the city, with high-density construction of thirty to forty units an acre to compensate for the high cost of clearing the land (since the CHA was bound by federally determined cost guidelines).[31]

The first head of the CHA was Elizabeth Wood. Wood was born in Japan, the daughter of an Episcopal missionary; perhaps it was her father's ethos that guided her work as leader of the agency. She was well respected by her staff for being detached from the corruption and patronage that plagued other arenas of city politics, and for being a committed proponent of fair housing. Wood believed that as a public institution the CHA could spur social change; her director of tenant selection observed that her beliefs "were formed by the Depression and the New Deal, which simply involved doing something for the people who were temporarily down on their luck," while her director of planning said she "believed in public agencies being catalytic agents outside the narrow field of their assigned jobs."[32] Given Wood's leadership, there was a chance in its early years that the CHA could offer an opportunity to erode the city's severe racial segregation. However, despite her belief in the social power of the new public institution in her care, Wood also feared reprisals from white families or even a resurgence of the violence Chicago saw in the infamous five-day race riot of 1919. She declared that the CHA "would not permit a housing project to change the racial make-up of the neighborhood in which it is located."[33]

Meanwhile, the city's political leaders also helped ensure that CHA construction would perpetuate segregation rather than challenge it. White members of the city council engaged in "aldermanic horse trading" where throughout the 1950s CHA officials proposed racially diverse sites for public housing construction

TABLE 1. Chicago Housing Authority projects in Bronzeville

Name	Location	Number of units	Year constructed
Ida B. Wells Homes and Extension	Pershing (Thirty-Ninth) and King Drive; Thirty-Seventh and Vincennes	1,652; 647	1941; 1955
Dearborn Homes	Twenty-Seventh and State	800	1950
Harold L. Ickes Homes	Twenty-Second and State	803	1955
Stateway Gardens	Thirty-Fifth and State	1,644	1958
Robert Taylor Homes	State Street, Pershing to Fifty-Fourth	2,208	1962
Clarence Darrow Homes	Thirty-Eighth and Langley	479	1961
Madden Park Homes	Pershing and Ellis	452	1970

Sources: Chicago Housing Authority Statistical Reports; Hunt, *Blueprint for Disaster*.

only to have white aldermen negotiate internally to strike from the list any new developments slated to be built in white neighborhoods. This arrangement allowed the CHA to maintain with a sort of plausible deniability that it was not intentionally promoting segregation, holding up its initially diverse lists as evidence that it intended to integrate.[34] This strategy was roundly criticized by Richard B. Austin, the judge who ruled in *Gautreaux v. Chicago Housing Authority*, filed in 1966 as a class action segregation suit:

> It is incredible that this dismal prospect of an all-Negro public housing system in all-Negro areas came about without the persistent application of a deliberate policy to confine public housing to all Negro or immediately adjacent changing areas. . . . No criterion, other than race, can plausibly explain the veto of over 99½% of the housing units located on the White sites which were initially selected on the basis of CHA's expert judgment and at the same time the rejection of only 10% or so of the units on Negro sites.[35]

However, by the time the *Gautreaux* decision was handed down the CHA had already built thousands of units of densely concentrated public housing in Bronzeville (table 1).

CITY OF CHILDREN

As these public housing projects were being constructed, debates raged in the worlds of architecture and public policy about what design would be best for families. High-rise apartments allowed more people to live in a smaller space and were therefore more cost effective. Elizabeth Wood, criticizing high-rises in 1952, argued that they violated a child's natural "need for nearness to his mother," whereas with row houses "indoor-outdoor activity takes place closer to where the mother is at work. The child can keep in touch with her. She can hear him if he cries or gets into a fight."[36] However, federal cost restrictions kept the CHA from constructing row houses along the State Street Corridor. The CHA took other arguably drastic steps to stay below price caps. Some of these measures were extreme and left residents facing subpar living conditions—such as including only two elevators for nine hundred residents in the 1959 construction of the Robert Taylor Homes. It's hard to imagine that such planning would have been considered acceptable had the people destined to live in these buildings not been poor and black. When people criticize the birth of the CHA, many are quick to point out that such high density created the conditions for social disorder. But this density also affected residents' lives more indirectly: the high density of an especially young population had a cascading effect on the public school system. From the 1950s through the 1980s, the CHA transformed the black metropolis into a city of children. First, restrictive covenants, violence, and segregation had hemmed thousands of black Chicagoans into Bronzeville in the 1920s, 1930s, and 1940s. Now the CHA—through a combination of well-intentioned social policy and draconian federal policy—brought huge numbers of African American children into the confined area, at proportions far exceeding the rest of the city.

TABLE 2. Bronzeville public housing: Age and racial characteristics

Residential area (construction year)	Year	Population[a]	Percent black	Population under 18 years old	Percent under 18 years old
City of Chicago	1950	3,659,721	14	914,663	24.99
	1960	3,550,404	23	1,104,175	31.10
	1970	3,369,359	33	907,433	26.93
	1980	3,005,072	40	852,875	28.38
Ida B. Wells Homes and Extension (1941, 1955)	1950	6,949	100	3,771	54.27
	1960	9,361	100	5,774	61.68
	1970[b]	11,130	100	7,245	65.09
	1980	6,730	100	3,790	56.32
Dearborn Homes (1950)	1950	2,642	95	1,452	54.96
	1960	3,282	100	2,039	62.13
	1970	3,000	100	1,890	63.00
	1980	2,585	100	1,615	62.48
Harold L. Ickes Homes (1955)	1960	3,711	98	2,448	65.97
	1970	3,310	100[c]	2,305	69.64
	1980	2,675	100	1,670	62.43
Stateway Gardens (1958)	1960	7,927	100	5,302	66.89
	1970	7,145	100	5,025	70.33
	1980	6,075	100	4,160	68.48
Clarence Darrow Homes (1961)	1980	2,610	100	1,910	73.18
Robert Taylor Homes (1962)	1970	26,690	100	20,440	76.58
	1980	19,785	100	14,165	71.59
Madden Park Homes (1970)	1970	2,120	100	1,585	74.76

Sources: Chicago Housing Authority Statistical Reports; Chicago Statistical Abstract; 1990 Census of Population and Housing.

[a] All officially reported CHA residential populations should be considered underestimates, since on-the-ground surveys have historically reported significant numbers of squatters and "off the lease" residents.

[b] CHA-reported figures for this year include the Clarence Darrow Homes, annexed to Ida B. Wells in 1961.

[c] In fact, one of the Ickes Homes' 788 families in this year was white, making up less than 1 percent of the resident population.

When selecting tenants, the CHA favored large families and even excluded childless ones, arguing that children were the most important beneficiaries of public housing. This made sense in a way—families needing affordable three- and four-bedroom apartments were more likely to have trouble finding places to live on the

TABLE 3. Total population and density of children: Bronzeville vs. Chicago, 1930–90

		Bronzeville (3.384 square miles)[a]	City of Chicago (237 square miles)
1930	Total population	137,290	3,376,438
	Percent black	93.21	6.93
	Total children	33,451	1,107,467
	Total children per square mile	**9,885**	**4,673**
1940	Total population	156,380	3,396,808
	Percent black	96.65	8.18
	Total children	43,657	941,756
	Total children per square mile	**12,901**	**3,974**
1950	Total population	193,302	3,620,962
	Percent black	98.19	13.59
	Total children	54,434	991,063
	Total children per square mile	**16,086**	**4,182**
1960	Total population	132,361	3,550,404
	Percent black	96.40	22.89
	Total children	49,958	1,104,175
	Total children per square mile	**14,763**	**4,659**
1970	Total population	121,426	3,366,957
	Percent black	94.68	32.75
	Total children	54,664	907,433
	Total children per square mile	**16,154**	**3,829**
1980	Total population	89,441	3,005,072
	Percent black	94.29	39.83
	Total children	34,600	852,875
	Total children per square mile	**10,225**	**3,599**
1990	Total population	66,549	2,783,726
	Percent black	95.8	39.07
	Total children	25,527	809,484
	Total children per square mile	**7,543**	**3,416**

Source: Chicago Statistical Abstract
Note: Based on available data, for 1930 to 1950 total population and density of children includes youth aged 0 to 19. For 1960 to 1990, it includes youth aged 0 to 18.
[a] Based on figures from the Douglas and Grand Boulevard community areas.

private market.[37] This policy created a startlingly dense region of children and youth in a very small geographic area, setting the conditions for what would ultimately become a population bubble destined to burst (tables 2 and 3).

Although only a small number of Bronzeville residents lived in public housing at the outset—just 5 percent in 1950—by 1970, nearly half were living in CHA housing. And these residents were mostly young. Compared with Chicago overall, Bronzeville and its housing projects were stacked with children. While the city's proportion of children and youth remained at about one-third from 1950 into 1990, the population in Bronzeville's public housing skewed much younger—half, two-thirds, or in some cases even three-quarters of public housing residents were under eighteen.[38] And from a spatial perspective, the community was just as remarkable in its numbers of children. At one point Bronzeville held, packed within its narrow borders, the astonishing figure of over 16,000 children per square mile—over four times the density of children in the city overall.

And every one of them, of course, would need a place to go to school.

"WE BUILD SCHOOLS WHERE THERE ARE STUDENTS"

> There are only two things of which the Chicago schools have always had more than enough—children and crises!
>
> —Mary J. Herrick, *The Chicago Schools: A Social and Political History*

Faced with such a monumental concentration of children, public officials and community members made efforts to bring them public resources, such as federally funded preschools and a tutoring program; they even converted spare apartments in the Harold L. Ickes Homes and Robert Taylor Homes into miniature branches of the public library system. But whatever they did, they were met with so much demand that there were always more young people than could be accommodated. By 1962 CHA officials were writing to their counterparts in the federal government requesting assistance for more playgrounds, because children at the Robert Taylor Homes were lining up "seven and eight deep just waiting to use a piece of play equipment."[39] One resident recalled this frustration from a child's perspective: "I'd have this ice cream cone in my hand, you know, that I'd bought from the ice cream man, and I wanted to wait till I got on the merry-go-round to eat it. But the line was around the block for one merry-go-round! Every day, all day and night. That ice cream would just melt down my hand before I could get on."[40]

And just as their parents and grandparents had been kept in Bronzeville by the invisible fence of segregation, the children of Bronzeville could not attend school just anywhere. They too were bound by the color line.

As soon as black families began arriving in the Great Migration, school officials fretted over what to do with them. Board of education member Max Loeb wrote an open letter in the *Defender* in 1918, wondering aloud if formally segregated schools might be the best way to address the increasing numbers of black children. "The colored population has increased largely since the War. Colored attendance in public schools has grown accordingly. How best can the Race antagonism be avoided which so often springs up when the two races are brought into juxtaposition?"[41]

In response to complaints of inequality, board of education president James McCahey blamed the problems on material limitations caused by World War II and "the housing trouble on the Near South Side," without which "the schools would be in top shape."[42] The solution, in the eyes of the board, was to build more schools in the areas of black population growth. In the meantime, McCahey argued, black Chicagoans should be grateful for their improved fortunes: no longer would children attend the dilapidated shacks that served as schools for African Americans in Mississippi, and "ordinarily, children from other states would be required to pay tuition," whereas the recent migrants were not. Further, McCahey insisted, the board had done nothing to intentionally create segregated school boundaries, and it was an unfortunate reality that no vacant seats existed in other parts of the city where black students might be able to enroll. Just happenstance—a matter of bad luck.

In response, Edwin Embree, chair of the Mayor's Committee on Race Relations, stated, "It is not a proper answer to point out that children receive a better education in Chicago than they do in rural Mississippi. . . . Education in Chicago must be judged by Chicago Standards."[43] Unfortunately, "Chicago Standards" included maintaining segregation at all costs. Rather than allow students to enroll in white schools, district officials created "double shifts" where black students attended school for only part of the day, then traded off with a second group. And just as they had done with housing, white Chicagoans made it very clear that they would not tolerate integrated schools. In 1945, two hundred white students at Englewood High School went on strike and their leaders besieged the assistant superintendent's office to complain about increasing black enrollment at their school.[44] Five hundred Morgan Park High School students convened to consider a strike but ultimately chose to petition the school board instead, requesting formally segregated schools.[45]

In 1948 the Supreme Court declared restrictive covenants illegal, and in the subsequent decade the density in Bronzeville eased somewhat. At the same time, Chicago got a new school leader, Herold C. Hunt, who was vocal in his willingness to address overcrowding and racial inequality in CPS. "Complete use of all buildings is the one principle I hope will govern all [attendance] boundary decisions," he said. "We have overcrowded schools in Negro areas, and vacant rooms and floors in neighboring schools that are predominantly white. Mixed schools exist in our system and no under-used school should be reserved as a white school."[46]

This administrative change in direction would not last, however. In 1953 Benjamin Willis became the head of CPS; he would hold the office for thirteen years, and his name would go down in history, perhaps more so than that of any other school leader in the city.

Willis was an avowed reformer who professed two core beliefs: that professional educators should be relied on to know what was best for schools and children, and the sanctity of the "neighborhood school."[47] He proclaimed no interest in politics, or in any effort to either segregate or integrate the schools, but simply set out to mirror the interests of each neighborhood—which, in a city beset by intense residential segregation, of course resulted in de facto school segregation. By drawing on the noble rhetoric of the neighborhood school and local control, Willis was able to effectively wash his hands of any accountability for systemic patterns across CPS. It was easy for him to declare a color-blind philosophy, partially because CPS was not required to collect any racial demographic information, allowing him to proclaim that he did not even *know*, or care to know, how many students of which racial backgrounds were attending which schools. (The Illinois legislature would not require the collection of such data until 1963.)

Local black leaders were not convinced. In 1958 the NAACP published an article in its journal the *Crisis*, "De Facto Segregation in the Chicago Public Schools," drawing on the implications of the recent *Brown v. Board* decision to argue that school leaders were responsible for the segregation that resulted from their policies and practices, even if segregation was not civic law. Given that there was still no official data gathering on the matter, the authors also set out to document the nature and extent of school segregation in the city. They argued that black students were assigned less experienced teachers and attended more crowded schools, and that the district's decisions were directly at the root of the matter. For instance, Bronzeville's DuSable High School "was built and districted to be Negro at a time when there were white schools east, west, and south of it." Without a doubt, the report concluded, "the Chicago Board of Education maintains in practice what amounts to a racially discriminatory policy."[48]

Willis's response to these accusations presages the defense Byrd-Bennett would make fifty-five years later. Although they were separated by their race, their background, and several decades, they mounted almost identical defenses while occupying the same role. Willis called segregation "a circumstantial thing" (another version of Byrd-Bennett's assertion that school closings' disproportionate impact on black students was "not racist, simply a fact") and stated that the district was "not concerned with race when we build new schools. We build schools where there are students." Alvin Rose, executive director of the CHA, made an analogous claim to race-blindness: "It is essential to plan housing units for areas where there is a need for them. We can't help it if whites move out when Negroes move in. . . . What can we do, force people to live in a certain place to integrate the area and the schools there? It's impossible." The real problem, Willis declared, was the overcrowding, caused by unforeseen demographic changes: the continued population growth among black students, which had been predicted to ebb after World War II.[49] Willis and his supporters said that accusations of racial discrimination were nonsense and a distraction from the district's need to respond urgently to demographic shifts. The solution, Willis said, was to build schools. Build many schools, and build them fast. Local media began referring to Willis as "Ben the Builder" as he oversaw the construction or major expansion of 208 elementary schools and 13 high schools over his tenure.[50]

In 1960 the CHA notified CPS that the school district should expect an enrollment increase of over ten thousand students in the area surrounding the Robert Taylor Homes, to be completed in 1962. Willis announced the construction of three new schools, displeasing black parents who felt that "new schools in Negro areas had been put there to perpetuate segregation. Their location seemed to be based on continued containment within the ghetto, particularly when the system took no action to promote integration."[51] And there was another problem. A Chicago Urban League researcher was informed by CHA whistleblowers that Willis's plans would accommodate only 7,765 students rather than the 10,000 forecast.[52] When the researcher complained to the school board, CPS retorted that the estimate of 10,000 students was overblown and that the planned schools could seat as many as forty students in each classroom—a slap in the face to parents and community members demanding higher-quality education. And, CPS argued, additional students could be accommodated in auxiliary trailers, and ground-floor CHA apartments could be converted into extra classrooms. Between the trailers and the idea of forty children to a room, CPS seemed to be admitting that subpar conditions for black students were just fine and that the top priority was to keep them in segregated schools within segregated neighborhoods.

Meanwhile, despite their overcrowding, schools for black students were receiving less funding per student than white schools, as well as more substitutes rather than experienced teachers and lower allocations for maintenance and operations. When board members requested an accounting of all unused spaces to assess possibilities for reallocation, they were met with what historian and former CPS teacher Mary J. Herrick calls "frustrating postponements and unclear figures":

> Some unused rooms in white schools were still not listed, as they were assigned to extra services (such as nurses) for which the Negro schools had no comparable space. . . . Busing children at public expense, a practice in use in several large Northern cities, was ruled out by a majority of the Board as too expensive. . . . [Willis] felt that the established pattern of neighborhood schools should not and could not be changed.[53]

Before long, tensions were flaring between district leaders and black Chicagoans. In 1961 a coalition of civil rights groups began Operation Transfer, in which they attempted to enroll black children in white schools with vacancies, knowing they would be turned away, but providing further evidence of the district's discriminatory practices. In 1962 four black mothers entered a school to see for themselves how many vacant spaces there were; they were arrested and found guilty of trespassing.[54] Parents lay down in the dirt overnight to prevent bulldozers from preparing the ground for more trailers, which they derisively called "Willis Wagons."[55] These actions were the Civil Rights–era predecessors of the direct activism described in chapter 1, which we might consider inspiring—or discouraging. More than five decades apart, black people in the same communities found themselves protesting the same problems. Not only did the district's actions show a disregard for black children, but the murkiness of the "process" supposedly in place added another layer of difficulty.

For weeks, students and parents marched and protested against Willis, culminating in a mass walkout on October 22, 1963, designated as "Freedom Day" by local activists and organizers. More than 220,000 students stayed out of school (about

48 percent of the total district), many marching in the streets or attending community-organized Freedom Schools in churches across the city. "KEEP YOUR CHILDREN OUT OF SCHOOL for this one day! Let them know you want a better future for them," exhorted one flyer. "Help us put an end to inferior, overcrowded schooling! Help to end the ruinous segregation of our children!" A flyer for another boycott, to be held June 10 and 11, 1965, decried a system "run by a Board that has FAILED to desegregate Chicago Schools" and asked, "Are we afraid of missing two days of NOTHING??"[56]

The *Defender* called Willis "the Gov. Wallace of Chicago standing in the doorway of an equal education for all Negro kids in this city—a one-man educational John Birch Society, incarnate and inviolate."[57] One *Defender* cartoon referred to the superintendent as "Massa Ben Willis."[58]

In 1964 the board commissioned five researchers led by Philip Hauser, head of the sociology department at the University of Chicago, to prepare a report on segregation in the district. Hauser and his team made several recommendations that seemed to defy CPS's official stance of "we can't help it." The researchers recommended that the district provide free transportation for students from overcrowded schools to schools with space and build new schools and draw attendance boundaries in ways that would foster integration, given that 90 percent of black students were attending schools that were at least 90 percent black.[59] Hauser also argued that there were 26,000 vacant seats immediately available where black students could be transferred, while Willis claimed there were only 12,809.

The recommendations of the Hauser report went unfulfilled.

Of course, Willis was not acting in a political vacuum. He was overseen by Mayor Richard J. Daley. Unlike his southern counterparts, Daley supported segregation simply by arguing fervently that it didn't exist. At an NAACP convention in 1963, the mayor said the city of Chicago had no ghettos; when a reporter asked what he thought was meant by the term, he responded shrewdly, "You could debate the semantics of ghettos for several years."[60] Mayor Daley's expressed school policy was to do "what the people want," perhaps undergirding Willis's focus on individual neighborhood schools rather than citywide concerns.[61] This was also a surefire strategy to appease white voters, some of whom he had lost in the 1963 election. In 1965, when community organizers filed a civil rights complaint alleging that CPS maintained racist practices, the district faced the loss of federal funding, which the Federal Civil Rights Act of 1964 specified could not be disbursed to discriminatory programs. In response, Mayor Daley held a personal meeting with President Lyndon B. Johnson, negotiating the eventual release of the funds.[62] But whether Willis himself was the architect of the plan or whether he was simply following orders from above, the facts were clear: CPS was keeping the black children of Bronzeville firmly in place. As their numbers grew, they were not able to fan out across the city. Instead, the schools they attended became more numerous and more crowded. And this was not happenstance, but a matter of policy.

Beginning in the late 1960s and into the 1970s, black political leaders, parents, and community organizers began to shift their political focus, in part reflecting broader trends across the country. Rather than focusing on school integration—especially busing that could put children at the center of harassment and danger—education organizers began emphasizing the need for agency and self-determination: the need to hire more black teachers and ensure that they got full-time positions and were not just substitutes, the need for black studies in the curriculum and community control of black schools, the need for black representation in the teachers' union, and so on.[63] At the same time, many white parents were taking their children out of CPS altogether. Although this period is notorious for the broader trend of "white flight" as many white residents across the country moved from urban centers to the suburbs, the decline in white public school enrollment far outpaced the decline in the city's white population, as many white families who remained enrolled their children in private or parochial schools.[64] Like the growth of the black student population, white students' departure from the system occurred considerably faster than expected. A 1967 report predicted that by 1980 CPS would have a white student population of 34.7 percent. By 1982, the actual proportion was 16.3 percent.[65]

In 1980 it seemed things might finally change. CPS—like the CHA with *Gautreaux* fourteen years earlier—found its racially discriminatory practices facing a legal challenge. The US Department of Justice alleged that the district was illegally segregating students through practices that included creating and altering school attendance boundaries, adjusting grade structures, failing to institute "educationally sound measures to relieve student overcrowding," maintaining "severely overcrowded and thereby educationally inferior schools in such a way as to identify . . . those schools as intended for Black students and less crowded schools as intended for white students," permitting white students to transfer easily to avoid their assigned schools in favor of majority-white schools, and allowing "the association of segregated schools with segregated housing projects."[66] The Justice Department claimed these practices were illegal and unconstitutional, "resulting in immediate, severe and irreparable harm." To address these allegations rather than go to trial, the district entered into a consent decree, committing to desegregate as many schools as possible.

In theory, this was supposed to be the tool that could finally change the face of CPS. No longer would black students be hemmed into certain schools that would just grow and grow while white schools sat empty. But things didn't pan out that way. In 2009 the consent decree was dissolved, with the court determining that CPS had made good-faith efforts to comply in the preceding decades. Arguably this dissolution had more to do with the changing demographics of the district—which by then enrolled only 9 percent white students—than with the achievement of desegregation. The consent decree never said Chicago schools had to be diverse, only that the district must strive for the "greatest practicable number of stably desegregated schools, considering all circumstances in Chicago." With dwindling numbers of white students in the system, the bar for creating an "integrated" school district had been lowered. That year the average black student in the Chicago region attended a school where 13.3 percent of the population was white, leading the authors of a report from UCLA's Civil Rights Project to call Chicago "noteworthy for its extremely unequal schools and virtually no effort to offset the problems."[67]

In short, during the years when Chicago's segregated housing concentrated remarkable numbers of children in Bronzeville, the city's segregated school system kept them from going elsewhere for their education. As new projects went up, so did the number of children attending the area's schools—and in the coming years, as the walls of CHA residences came tumbling down, so did CPS enrollment.

PARADISE LOST AND THE PLAN FOR TRANSFORMATION

At this point the Black Metropolis had become a city of children. But Bronzeville's reality as a high-density enclave of children attending crowded schools was not to last forever—because the high-rise public housing that was home to so many of them was destined to come down.

The 1970s and 1980s saw a troubling shift in the world of Bronzeville's projects and the rest of the city's public housing. From former residents to journalists, everyone seemed to have a theory: poverty, gang violence, unemployment, a "culture of poverty," the influx of crack cocaine, the departure of the black middle class. Everyone has a theory, and they all believe that theory explains why public housing failed. Even gang members active at the time blame *other* gangs.[68] Whatever the reason, public housing was no longer the idyllic dream of those early Ida B. Wells days. One resident described visiting the Dearborn Homes where he had grown up: "About 1984 or 1985—I came back and I just walked through Dearborn Homes. It was eleven-thirty, twelve at night, and I went up to the apartment that I had lived in. The elevators were broken, so I walked up the stairs to see what it's like today. It's horrible, it's terrible. I couldn't imagine anybody living there."[69]

In 1986 the *Chicago Tribune* ran an eleven-part series called "The Chicago Wall," detailing the CHA's troubling story. The "wall" referred to the State Street Corridor as "a physical and psychological barrier that divides the city in an abundance of ways and stands as a perverse monument to decades of misdirected public policy and race-conscious political decision-making."[70] Describing the State Street Corridor, Theophilus Mann—then the only African American member of the CHA board—commented, "We have extended this ghetto too far, and I think it is going to have repercussions when I am gone. I think someone will come out and spit on my grave because I should have done something."[71]

The projects' dense youth population presented particular challenges as CHA officials struggled to keep up with physical maintenance. Lacking adequate safe places to play, children amused themselves in stairwells, in lobbies, in hallways—and above all, in elevators. "We used to ride them like we was at [Six Flags] Great America. Popping them buttons, loading as many kids as we could, trying to climb out of them if we could."[72] This put children in danger and worsened living conditions for residents relying on the elevators to get in and out of their high-rise apartments.[73] A report from the US Department of Housing and Urban Development criticized CHA management, proclaiming that "no one seems to be minding the store; what's more, no one seems to genuinely care."[74]

National attention on the CHA and its residents fueled further social stigma. A *New York Times* editorial titled "What It's Like to Be in Hell" painted a grim portrait: the author, described as a "a New York lawyer who recently visited Chicago's housing projects," misspelled the name of the street where the project he visited was located: "The illusions end on Damon [*sic*] Street. . . . Firefights may erupt at any time. Children dodge machine-gun crossfire as they leave the school. Sudden bullets smash through windows into apartment walls. Watch the residents walk; they have the affinity for ground of seasoned infantry soldiers."[75]

In 1999 Mayor Richard M. Daley negotiated with the Department of Housing and Urban Development to take back control of CHA, which had been seized by the federal government three years before.[76] HUD agreed that the CHA, under new mayoral supervision, would demolish nearly 22,000 units—including all the high-rises—and build or renovate an additional 25,000 units over ten years at the cost of $1.56 billion.[77] Mayor Daley announced that the CHA would be completely overhauled—an effort that would take a decade: the Plan for Transformation (simply, the Plan) was born. The CHA touted it as socially symbolic, going beyond physical changes to the city's housing stock: "[The Plan] aims to build and strengthen communities by integrating public housing and its leaseholders into the larger social, economic and physical fabric of Chicago. . . . Where there were once isolated superblocks, the street grid is being recreated to seamlessly integrate the new developments into the surrounding neighborhoods."[78] In other words, the CHA promised to tear down the invisible fence. Mayor Daley swore he wanted to do more than rebuild residents' homes: "I want to rebuild their souls."[79]

The Plan granted a "right of return" to 26,199 households, meaning the families displaced by the demolition could be granted space in new or redeveloped residences or given affordable housing vouchers. As of March 2010, fewer than half of these households remained in the system: only 5,755 families and 46 senior citizens lived in new or renovated CHA sites, with an additional 2,217 seniors in specially designated senior housing; another 4,060 families and 231 seniors received vouchers to find privately owned affordable housing elsewhere in the city.[80] Additionally, those families who did return had to meet a variety of eligibility requirements to stay within the CHA system, from a mandate that they work thirty hours a week to provisions that they have adequate child care, maintain a good credit rating, and be subject to drug screening and background checks.[81]

And just like that, the Black Metropolis was a city of children no more. From 1990 to 1995, Bronzeville lost 272 children; from 1995 to 2000, it lost over 6,000.[82] Naturally, this meant that schools saw major drops in enrollment. From 1989 to 2000, Bronzeville school enrollments dipped an average of 20 percent (table 4). A 2007 report from the University of Chicago's Chapin Hall noted that Bronzeville had lost a large part of its child population between 1990 and 2005 and predicted that such drops would continue at least through 2010, with the northern end of the community in particular projected to lose 27 to 40 percent of its children. The authors of the report also pointed out that, citywide, "school closings do not map exactly onto child and youth

TABLE 4. Bronzeville elementary schools: Enrollment and closures

		Annual enrollment								
School	Location	1989	1990	1991	1992	1993	1994	1995	2000	Closure
Attucks	3813 S. Dearborn	716	642	645	623	609	673	630	441	Moved to Farren in 2008; closed in 2015
Donoghue	707 E. 37th	750	701	681	762	743	775	784	611	2003
Doolittle Intermediate	535 E. 35th	499	509	573	538	496	460	452	415	Open
Doolittle West	521 E. 35th	876	879	916	774	701	684	666	681	2004
Douglas	3200 S. Calumet	602	568	581	552	574	549	550	621	2004; in 2005 Pershing West moves in
Drake	2722 S. King Drive	412	382	368	410	381	365	388	388	Open; relocated to former Williams building
Einstein	3830 S. Cottage Grove	505	470	465	456	511	441	398	—	1999
Farren	5055 S. State	906	886	838	831	787	802	787	430	2006; Attucks moves in 2008
Fuller	4214 S. St. Lawrence	542	549	588	556	522	539	468	444	Entered "turnaround" process in 2012
Mayo	249 E. 37th	682	638	628	614	587	591	576	497	2013
McCorkle	4421 S. State St.	545	490	509	483	537	549	470	360	2010
Mollison	4415 S. King Drive	501	473	444	499	528	550	511	514	Open
Overton	221 E. 49th	1,021	979	915	900	870	835	873	787	2013
Pershing [East]	3113 S. Rhodes Ave.	288	279	267	276	273	268	274	269	Open; becomes Pershing East in 2005; moves to Pershing West/Douglas building in 2013
Pershing West (opens 2005)	3200 S. Calumet	—	—	—	—	—	—	—	—	2013
Raymond	3663 S. Wabash	814	813	809	801	761	823	783	583	2004
Woodson North	4414 S. Evans	434	369	363	340	335	372	346	343	2003; reopened as charter
Woodson South	4414 S. Evans	672	548	550	501	433	569	534	518	Entered "turnaround" process in 2012

Sources: Chicago Public Schools Data Books; *Chicago Tribune*; Chicago Public Schools 2011 Transition Report; *Catalyst Chicago*.

population losses." For instance, the gentrifying West Town community (where in 2000 only about 9 percent of residents were black) saw the largest numerical drop in child and youth population but no school closings[83]—suggesting that the "underutilization crisis" was considered a crisis only when it happened in certain neighborhoods.

The Plan for Transformation has forever changed the face of the city—especially the South Side—and leaves seemingly endless questions.[84] But one thing seems certain: the demolition of public housing in Bronzeville dealt the community's schools a jolt from which they perhaps never recovered. For instance, sociologists found that four years after the demolition of the Robert Taylor Homes, about a quarter of the families they spoke with kept their children in their old schools near Robert Taylor because they hoped to maintain relationships with teachers they trusted. Parents scattered across the city by the demolition sometimes even sent their children to live with relatives back in the old neighborhood to keep them at the same schools.[85] This is a story we have heard over and over: that far from being interchangeable, the relationships children and families form in schools are important and difficult to replace. But these relationships and this history—the culmination of a century of segregation that fenced people in, then suddenly forced them out—goes unacknowledged in an official district narrative that refers to "underutilization" as something that simply happens—an act of nature.

HISTORY HIDDEN IN PLAIN SIGHT

> As the CHA gets out of the business of housing the poor, it's only a matter of time before CPS gets out of the business of educating their children. It's almost as if that were the plan all along.
>
> —Ben Joravsky, *Chicago Reader*

In an interview with Martin, an eighteen-year-old Bronzeville resident who has seen both his grammar school and his high school close. I startle myself when I do the math and realize he may be too young to recall life before the Plan for Transformation. I ask if he remembers the projects. He tells me he doesn't, but says he knows where they all were. "You can't ride around this area with my parents or with any older adults without them pointing it out, telling you, 'this right here, this used to be Ida B. Wells! This used to be . . . !'" In the minds of many Bronzeville residents, vivid memories remain of the CHA high-rises and the large-scale public housing that once dominated the physical and social space of the community. And yet, in the official justifications for school closures issued by CEO Barbara Byrd-Bennett, Mayor Rahm Emanuel, and others representing the district and the city, there was no acknowledgment of the role the Plan for Transformation may have played in enrollment declines. This is strange, because Mayor Rahm Emanuel, the vocal public advocate for the closures and in many ways the overseer of the school district (given that CPS's CEO, school board, and board president are all mayoral appointees) was vice-chairman of the CHA from 1999 to 2001. Emanuel had a singular perspective on the Plan and the way it might affect the rest of the city—including its schools. Segregation, restrictive covenants, Willis Wagons, demolition of public housing—these policies all laid the groundwork for the present reality of empty schools dotting the landscape. They are not obscure facts; they are front and center in the minds of the people who lived this history. But in the eyes of the district it's as if they never happened.

This absence is especially notable when one considers the claim that the 2013 school closures were color-blind, race-neutral, or otherwise not racist; an honest discussion about the history of the CHA and CPS in Bronzeville, in particular, would have necessitated a tacit admission that both agencies were complicit in constructing the "invisible fence"—the social boundary that kept Bronzeville's schools and housing deeply segregated throughout the twentieth century. Contrary to the statements from Byrd-Bennett, in Bronzeville "underutilization" of schools has *everything* to do with race.

The school closures that took place in Bronzeville in 2013 were a policy rooted in racism. These actions were not racist because of the "hearts and minds" of the people who made the decisions; I don't know these people and can't claim to know their hearts or their minds, and in any case that would be beside the point. They were racist because they were the culmination of several generations of racist policy stacked on racist policy, each one disregarding, controlling, and displacing black children and families in new ways layered upon the callousness of the last. Somewhere, in an alternate universe, I imagine that Barbara Byrd-Bennett made an honest statement in front of the board of education. It went something like this:

> The schools in Bronzeville do not have as many children as they once did. Once upon a time Bronzeville was so besieged by overcrowding that its schools' being empty would have seemed inconceivable. But empty school buildings did not arise spontaneously. From the violent bombings and restrictive covenants that kept those who arrived in the Great Migration hemmed into Bronzeville, to CHA site selection that succumbed to the limitations of racism and politics in Chicago and thereby perpetuated segregation rather than integration, to Willis-era policies that maintained segregated and overcrowded schools, to a Plan for Transformation that displaced many thousands of Bronzeville residents in a very short period and has made it difficult for

> them to return home, the story of the community's empty school buildings has deep roots in history. Sadly, that history is a racist history. Now we are tasked to do something about it.

Alas, that isn't the statement we got on this plane of existence.

For much of the twentieth century and into the present, for black residents Chicago has been a city of precariousness, of uncertainty, of loss. And none of the history discussed in this chapter is a secret. While the account given here certainly includes some policy details and retroactive analysis, much of the story played out in high-profile ways: in community meetings, in giant headlines, in hallways, in the streets. Nor are these memories especially distant. In many ways the "underutilized" schools of 2013 are the descendants of educational policies made within my parents' lifetime, or in some cases in my own or even those of my middle school students. So when this history goes undiscussed by a public official, it reinforces what many black Chicagoans already believe to be true: that school leaders are untrustworthy, that they do not have the best interests of black children in mind, and that they talk out both sides of their mouths. Furthermore, this history dictates that if the district has any hope of becoming an institution dedicated to social justice, it is only through tireless struggle in a seemingly endless fight.

And then there's the matter of why we came here in the first place. In Bronzeville these struggles are about more than the denial of high-quality affordable housing or the violation of civil rights, even more than the city's abdication of its responsibility to provide children with a high-quality education. The troubling history of racism in housing and schooling as paired institutions in the community—at once parallel and circling one another like the strands of a double helix—is an affront to the aspirations of those black migrants who came north a century ago, to their flight from the violence and the indignities of life in the Jim Crow South, to the hope in their hearts when they called out, in the words of Richard Wright, "Good God Almighty! Great Day in the Morning! It's here! Our time has come! We are leaving! We are angry no more; we are leaving! We are bitter no more; we are leaving!" Those first black residents came to Chicago in search of freedom; they made a home where they could and called it Bronzeville. Whether Bronzeville can, in the century to come, continue to be a home for their great-grandchildren, and the children of those children, remains to be seen.

3 *Dueling Realities*

> Children see things very well sometimes—and idealists even better.
>
> —Joseph Asagai in *A Raisin in the Sun*, by Lorraine Hansberry

They called his name, and as the judge listened and the court reporter took notes, Bronzeville resident Trey Barksdale[1] took the microphone and made his statement.

> I'm not gonna waste too much time rehashing the same things. But there's one thing I need to state. That it sounds like a broken record, like we keep hitting our head against the wall. These consolidations and closings are racist. Plain and simple, clear and cut. [In] '63 my mother and my grandmother fought against the first Daley to get a better life and a better education. And yet, fifty years later, we're still doing the same thing. So, we give you data. Teachers, professionals, they're giving data over and over again how to improve schooling for our children. Especially children of color. Arts, music programs, physical education, rehabbing of buildings. And yet we've given you this information and you've not done anything about it. So it kind of seems like to me you really don't care. 'Cause you don't.

Despite the official trappings of a legal ordeal, this was not a trial—it was a public hearing to determine the fate of Overton Elementary School. In 2013, once CPS announced the list of fifty-four schools slated for closure, a series of hearings were held to present the district's justifications for the closure and allow members of the public to offer commentary and feedback. Each hearing was designated to be two hours long and was presided over by a "hearing officer," a retired judge tasked with reviewing the evidence presented and making a recommendation to the CEO on whether the school should be closed. A court reporter recorded the proceedings, and people were assured that questions would be answered a few days later on a district website. Representatives from the district began each meeting by reading prepared statements, then a CPS attorney presented a statement. The attorneys each had a binder of data, which they referred to as "exhibits" like evidence at a trial: "At this time I would like to tender to you the CEO's compiled exhibit one, a binder of documents being submitted for your consideration in support of these proposals. . . . The binder consists of documentary evidence in written statements demonstrating [that] the CEO's proposals comply with the requirements of the Illinois school code and the CEO's guidelines for school actions." Then community members (if they registered in advance) were able to take the microphone and make their comments.

A judge, an opening statement, a court reporter, the words "hearing" (not community meeting, or town hall, or open forum), "exhibit one"—these events sure seemed like a trial, with each school acting as defendant. How could they not? When we enter a social situation, we rely on cues and learned "scripts" to understand what behavior is expected of us. The way we speak and act will be different at a conference, in a classroom, at a town hall meeting, or at a church service. Although the closure hearings were not actual trials, their structure made them appear to be exactly that, leaving children, teachers, and parents to defend themselves, each other, and their school.

How do you judge a school, an institution of organized human relationships? What makes a good school? The answer has varied over time. During the era of mass immigration to the United States from Eastern Europe, a "good" school would teach students American norms, language, and values. During the Cold War, a "good" school prepared students to take an active role in standing against Soviet influence.[2] What does it mean to be a good school in a black neighborhood in Chicago in the first half of the twenty-first century?

In chapter 2 we explored why people care about "failing" institutions by looking at schools on a communitywide historical scale. We saw the ways racism and the policies of the CHA and CPS created an element of social instability for black families, who over the twentieth century had to cope with overcrowded and substandard housing, then the loss of public housing, as well as with overcrowded schools and the need to expend significant political energy demanding something better from CPS. Fifty years later, as Trey Barksdale pointed out, they found themselves in the same situation. In this chapter we will pivot back to the twenty-first century and move to a much smaller scale to consider the implications of that history and those experiences: a world in which the CPS officials charged with running schools and the black students, teachers, and parents affiliated with those schools occupy largely divergent realities. With those dueling realities come dueling belief systems and ideologies regarding how a school ought to be assessed and its future determined.

This chapter will focus on three schools in Bronzeville that CPS determined were failing. Community members showed up and spoke out to argue that this was not the truth—and that CPS's history as untrustworthy made district leaders unfit even to understand what a good school looks like. From beyond the Veil, these schools look irredeemable. But for those within the Veil, there's more to the story.

We have already seen one example of these dueling realities embodied in Barbara Byrd-Bennett's statement about the school closures. Byrd-Bennett is a black woman, and when she took her position as the head of CPS she already had a long list of credentials as an educator. In a career spanning three decades, she had been a teacher, a principal, and a district leader in New York, Detroit, and Cleveland and had been the chief education officer at CPS. When she defended the proposed closures at a hearing in April 2013, she brought these identities to the fore, inviting listeners to see her as someone who couldn't possibly be guilty of the racism alleged against her. "To refuse to challenge the status quo that is failing thousands of African-American students year after year," she said, "consigning them to a future with less opportunities than others—now, that's what I call racist. I grew up and went to school in an overwhelming African-American community where the schools were underutilized and under-resourced. So believe me—I *know* what racism is, and what racism is not."

As we will see, this issue—"what racism is, and what racism is not"—is far more contestable than Byrd-Bennett would lead us to believe. Indeed, as I will argue, the very language she uses in her statement, and the language other CPS officials use, is not a matter of clear-cut definitions and facts. Each statement is a claim about schools and their value.

The three "failing" Bronzeville elementary schools were all similar demographically, historically, and academically (see table 5). William J. and Charles H. Mayo Elementary School, opened in 1951 and named after the founders of the Mayo Clinic, was intended to demonstrate family-community partnership to the rest of the district, including programs for parents to observe

TABLE 5. Selected characteristics of focal schools, 2012–13

School	Opened	Enrollment	Percent black	Percent receiving special education services	Percent receiving free/reduced lunch
Mayo	1951	408	92.9[a]	8.3	94.6
Overton	1963	431	91.9[b]	8.1	95.4
Williams	1952	383	98.4	16.4	90.9

Source: Chicago Public Schools, *School data*, 2016.
[a] District data reports for Mayo indicate 1 percent of students ($n = 4$) reporting as Latino and 6.1 percent "not available."
[b] District data reports for Overton indicate 1.2 percent of students ($n = 5$) reporting as Latino and 6.7 percent "not available."

classroom learning and work with an in-house representative from the local YMCA.[3] Overton, opened in 1963, was named for Anthony Overton, leader of a successful cosmetics conglomerate and publisher of the *Chicago Bee*, the black newspaper that coined the term Bronzeville. The school's architecture was unique in the district; three three-story towers connected by corridors were designed to supply wide hallways and classrooms with ample natural light.[4] Williams, named after Daniel Hale Williams, the black doctor who was the first in the nation to perform open-heart surgery, was opened in 1952 to alleviate overcrowding at nearby Drake, where students were enrolled in double shifts.[5] The school building sits among the Dearborn Homes, the only high-rise public housing in Bronzeville that was renovated rather than demolished during the Plan for Transformation. All three schools served an almost entirely African American student population.[6]

SPEECH AS ACTION

When Barbara Byrd-Bennett says "I know what racism is, and what racism is not," she is not only *saying* something—she is also, through language, *doing* something. Speech, it turns out, is a form of action. What does that mean?

Imagine a store employee has mistreated you. You're upset, and you ask to speak to a manager. The employee takes you to the manager's office. When you open the door, the manager is sitting behind a desk. Before you can say anything, she says, "Would you like to have a seat?" Or perhaps she says, "Who are you and what are you doing in my office?" Or perhaps "Wow, I absolutely love your shirt. Where did you get it?" In each case, you would understand that she is not simply seeking information; her purpose is not just to learn whether you want to sit down, or who you are, or where you shop. Each of these questions is an attempt to *do* something: to calm you, or challenge you, or put you at ease. Each question is a *speech act*: she is saying something, but she is also making a social move. She is taking an action to move this moment between you in the direction she wants it to go.

Discourse analysis is a method for analyzing actions like these. It is a research method that asks, "When this person says this, what are they doing in the social space?" To better understand CPS school closing hearings, I used a particular variety known as *critical discourse analysis*. The "critical" part means I am paying attention to power, social relationships, inequality, and political institutions and the way they show up in spoken interactions so as to better understand the social conditions that produce those actions.

Before the public comment period of each closing hearing, CPS staff members read prepared statements. They are there not to represent themselves or their personal opinions but to give the official perspective of the district; they even preface their comments by saying "on behalf of the CEO." They repeatedly refer to specific guidelines that led to the closure proposal. In doing so they portray the decision as based on neutral, objective facts, not on any particular ideology or value bias. The first such statement is made by Brittany Meadows, who introduces herself as a "CPS portfolio planner." Her statement is a fill-in-the-blanks document: identical words for each school, with the respective data filled in as applicable:

> To understand the enrollment efficiency range of a facility, Chicago Public Schools utilizes its space utilization standards which are located in your binder at Tab 14. The enrollment efficiency range is plus or minus 20% of the facility's ideal enrollment. For elementary school buildings, the ideal enrollment is defined as the number of allotted homerooms multiplied by 30. The number of allotted homerooms is approximately 76 to 77% of the total classrooms available. . . . There are 31 total classrooms within the Mayo facility. Approximately 76 to 77% of 31 is 23, the number of allotted homerooms. Twenty-three multiplied by 30 yields the ideal enrollment of the facility, which is 690. As such, the enrollment efficiency range of the Mayo facility is between 552 and 828 students. As I stated, the enrollment of Mayo as of the 20th day of attendance for the 2012–2013 school year is 408. This number is below the enrollment efficiency range, and thus the school is underutilized.

To most educators or members of the broader public, the language Meadows uses would seem completely alien, detached from the school's day-to-day functioning. What is an "enrollment efficiency range"? Meadows's explanation of the term only provokes more questions. Why plus or minus 20 percent? Why is the ideal number thirty children per classroom? What on earth should we make of the bizarre "76 to 77 percent" idea? Although the binder containing her statement was available for attendees to review during the hearing, there was no opportunity to interact with the district representatives or question them directly. Community members were told that this meeting was for them to share *their* perspectives unidirectionally, not to have any sort of dialogue. In this sense the hearings were very much *not* like a trial. Or, rather, they were like a trial with no one to represent the defendant, no opportunity for cross-examination, and only one attorney permitted to review the evidence in advance.

Meadows closes with the language of logic: "This number is below the enrollment efficiency range, and *thus* the school is underutilized" (my emphasis). Meadows presents this data using an "if . . . then" statement, explaining the *calculation* of the metrics without explaining the *validity* of the constructs involved. In this manner the school closure proposal appears natural and inevitable. *Well, of course, since this number is below the enrollment efficiency range, this is what happens next.* Meadows is absolved of any personal responsibility for this decision. She is merely the messenger, delivering facts and numbers that can't be denied.

The logic implied in Meadows's statement reflects a certain view of reality: the idea that the most important aspects of the educational enterprise can easily be captured in no-nonsense, nondebatable numeric facts. These numbers are taken to be unbiased and a truer representation of what happens in a school building than more qualitative measures (teacher observations, for instance), which are seen as overly subjective or unreliable. These quantifiable facts are also seen as a necessity—perhaps an imperfect measure, but a needed force for decision making in school systems that serve thousands on thousands of students.[7] This idea is reflected in a common response to critiques of standardized testing: "They're not great, but we need to have *some* way of seeing how these schools are doing." As sociologist Wendy Espeland writes, "[Quantitative measures] have the patina of objectivity: stripped of rhetoric and emotion, they show what is 'really going on.' Even more, they can reduce vast amounts of information to a figure that is easy to understand, a simplicity that intimates that there is nothing to hide, and indeed that nothing can be hidden."[8]

In many situations such quantitative measures can of course be useful. But in this instance it seems inappropriate to rely on them so heavily, to the exclusion of other forms of knowledge or insight or subtlety, as the basis for a decision that will have a huge impact on hundreds of people's lives. In a sense, though, they reflect the culmination of a broader trend in education: an obsession with numbers to the exclusion of other forms of information and without the nuance or technical training needed to understand the real limitations of those numbers.[9] Daniel Koretz, a scholar considered an expert on standardized testing, notes that most Americans tend to overestimate how well such tests can provide a complete picture of academic success, especially schoolwide.

> When a school performs well or poorly on an achievement test, the reason can be the quality of education, any number of noneducational causes, or—more likely—both. Figuring out which is the case is not always easy. [Observers are] eager to infer school quality from the test scores alone, without doing the hard work of digging up the additional data one would need to identify differences in educational effectiveness. . . . People routinely misinterpret differences in test scores, commonly attributing more to quality of education than they ought.[10]

Koretz's cautionary words echo as we consider the statement of another district employee, Justin Brent. Like Meadows, Brent is charged with giving an identical statement at each of the hearings, with the appropriate numbers filled in. His task in this statement is to compare the test scores of the school being closed with the test scores of the "welcoming school" that students would be designated to attend. In this version of the statement, he compares the test scores of the closing school (Mayo) with those of the receiving school (Wells).

> Wells's ISAT [Illinois Standards Achievement Test] meets and exceeds composite score was 66.4, while Mayo's meets and exceeds composite score was 62.5. . . . As you can see, Wells's reading value-added score was a positive .4 in 2012 and Mayo's reading value-added score was -.7. This means that on average students at Wells grew at a faster pace in reading when compared to students at Mayo. Wells's mathematics value-added score was -.6 in 2012 [protest from audience]—I'm sorry, Well's mathematics value-added score was .6 in 2012, and Mayo's value-added score was -1.7. This means that on average, students at Wells grew fast—grew at a faster pace in mathematics when compared to students at Mayo. To summarize, Wells performed higher than Mayo in 2011–2012 on a majority of the metrics identified in the CEO's guidelines for school actions, and thus is a higher-performing school.

In a system that once refused to provide any information whatever about vacant schools and had parents arrested for attempting to find out for themselves, Meadows and Brent are presenting statements that are intended to ensure comparative transparency. They are not just pronouncing that one school is better than another but are giving a detailed explanation of *how* they came to their conclusions. But, of course, what is missing is any clear view of *why*. Why are these reasonable metrics to use in making a decision?

As Brent and Meadows present this particular view of reality, the structure of the event and the language they use makes it difficult to challenge them. They are not taking questions or comments, and they use the language of a mathematical algorithm. By the time we get to the "thus" that closes the statement, in order to agree that there is a causal logic—*x*, thus *y*—we also have to agree about other things: that the ISAT is a solid representation of educational quality; that value-added scores matter and that a difference of 2.3 points between two schools is a meaningful indicator that one is better than the other; that 2011–12 is the only year worth looking at to make this decision; that the CEO's guidelines for school actions are fair and reasonable. By implicitly presenting these questions as settled—as a given, as something we have all agreed on—district officials suggest that this is neutral evidence. We are to understand that these are the things that make a school good or bad and that this is beyond dispute, debate, or discussion.

However, when it's community members' turn to take the microphone, we hear a very different view of reality.

ANOTHER REALITY

The perspectives on three schools offered by teachers, students, community members, and parents could not be more different from district officials' neutral, matter-of-fact version of a quantitative reality. They present an entirely different picture of events, one informed by years of personal interaction with the school as well as an acknowledgment of broader contexts: the history of CPS, the history of Chicago and particularly of racism in the city, and the social significance of each school. It's not that community members dispute the facts of the "case": they don't go up the microphone and accuse the district officials of lying or dispute the numbers they have presented. Rather, they offer a different logic—a different reality, with a different understanding of what evidence should count in determining the value of a school and a different understanding of what racism is and the huge scale on which it functions.

CPS teachers, like teachers across the country, have been pushed to become amateur data analysts in the service of school "accountability" and "data-driven instruction." Teacher Nakia Mosby of Williams uses that experience to question whether the data analysis presented is sound, citing other numbers available from the state's performance data website and from a newspaper's annual ranking of schools. She suggests that a difference of a few points on one test is not sufficient evidence for closing a school:

> What information determines which school is higher performing or not? . . . I compared the two [school performance] report cards and even based on the *Sun-Times* you have Williams Middle as 67.3 and Drake as 69.9. Does that few points determine that they're a better school? It's just not enough information for the community, the parents, the teachers, everyone involved in this decision making. . . . You know we need to look at every single detail and not just one report card that's half done, missing data, missing information to make a critical decision like this. This is impacting people's lives, people's future, people's children. And I ask you all to look at this data. Do not look at one year's worth of data. Go back. It's right there.

Her comments hark back once again to the warning Koretz issued—the danger that district officials are too reliant on test scores to provide a 360-degree view of a school's educational quality.

One middle school student, Jordan McKendrick, begins her testimony by making a broad statement regarding school closures before moving on to speak directly to the case of Mayo:

> Hi, everybody, my name is Jordan McKendrick. Okay, so. This is not just for everybody. I feel like this is so racist of y'all to close down all these CPS schools because most—you see, most black

> kids going to CPS schools. It's taking away education from them when you closing their schools down and you movin' them into new schools and you takin' them out they comfort zone and you takin' jobs from teachers. That's not right. That's not fair at all. Okay, back to Mayo.

As discussed in chapter 2, during the 1950s and 1960s superintendent Benjamin Willis used a focus on the individual neighborhood school to deflect attention from racism; black political leaders and education organizers countered that focus by demanding he pay attention to systemwide patterns. Here a child takes that same stand. She is supposed to talk only about her school, but she subverts the structure of the hearing by insisting on making a statement regarding *all* of CPS—that school closures are racist because of their disproportionate impact on black children.

Carla Watts, a former principal, takes the point about racism even further, using a startling metaphor—the slave auction, where families were routinely separated for the expedience and economic gain of white slaveholders.

> So now we put [teachers] out to pasture when they have built all these skills for these children and now they're going to be put out there with other teachers trying to grapple for a job. I feel like I'm at a slave auction. I'm very full right now. Because I'm, like, begging you [begins to cry] to keep my family together. Don't take them and separate them.

At another point in her statement, Watts refers to the school and its students as "the fruits of my womb, my labor." Watts's plaintive request to keep her family together is echoed by many hearing participants. Many students, like Ke'Shaun Knowles, state that they consider their classmates brothers and sisters:

> My name is Ke'Shaun. And the reason I came up here today is for Mayo School to not close. 'Cause the school is like my home. And the teacher is like my, um, mother. And . . . the students like my brothers and sisters and my cousins. That's the reason I do not want Mayo School to close. Thank you.

When Ke'Shaun uses these words describing family bonds, it's more than a metaphor, given the importance of fictive kinship in African American social life. In African American social networks fictive kin often share the same rights, status, and intensity of relational bonds as biological kin.[11] Indeed, at the Williams hearing, Chicago Teachers Union representative Michael Lucas draws a connection between school closures, the historical challenges faced by African Americans, and his contemporary sense of responsibility for children who are not his own:

> This is real fast without taking into consideration real people, real babies, okay? So like I stated I have children. You know I don't have any grandchildren yet, but I'm sure hopefully I will. I want to be an advocate and continue to be an advocate for children or other folks' children just like my own. Because really I'm going to tell you something—I consider us a community, a family. Okay? We've come a long way. And again I'm not casting aspersions but we've come a long way from where we've began as African Americans. Coming over here from Africa and going through what we went through in terms of the slavery and our ancestors and so on and so forth. And then what we went through in the South and the North and then all of a sudden we do get *Brown versus Board of Education*, but the Supreme Court really doesn't really put any teeth in it, and what happened back then historically was that the schools in the South, many of them they shut them—they shut down the school districts.

In this narrative Lucas establishes a through line of concern, pain, and resilience, moving in conversational flow from his own children, his feelings of accountability for the children of others, and history from slavery to desegregation to the closure of black southern schools post-*Brown*—all as reasons Williams should remain open. For him this is relevant information, relevant evidence that should be used to inform this decision yet has not been acknowledged by anyone in power. Speaking from behind the Veil, he challenges a version of events that acts as if history never happened—as if the timeline of everything we need to know somehow begins with 2011 test scores.

In addition to such fictive kinship ties, community members refer to long-standing connections between biological family members and the school. Rayven Patrick, an eighth grader who says she has attended Mayo since preschool, discusses both forms of kinship seamlessly, intertwining them as she describes the rituals of daily school life and graduation. Like Lucas, she is talking about the importance of history, a history in which she and her family play an important role.

> Most of my family have went to Mayo. My grandma attended. My mother, my aunt. I came from a big family. The Patricks are known in Mayo. Like, we have been going there for so long. Over the years I have watched lots of students graduate, and they were able to come back to their teachers and tell them how high school has been going. Most of them are in college now, and I see them come to the few teachers that are left at Mayo and tell them of their experience of college and high school. This year I will graduate. And most of the students at Mayo, I think of them as my little sisters. They're family to me. Little sisters and little brothers. I walk through the hallway, and every kid knows who I am. I'm

> able to speak to them, and I honestly, I wanna be able to watch them graduate.

The recurrence of discourse around "family," both biological and fictive, is so prevalent during the hearings that one speaker at the Mayo hearing, DeMarcus Johnson, makes an explicit observation about it:

> Now, one of the things that I have looked at from after the first speech to the final speech is that this school is based on family. And I know because as I stated I have four decades of it. To tear down this family will be one of the biggest mistakes that Chicago Public Schools has done in years. And the reason why I say that is because we have the Johnson family, we have the Patrick family, we have the McKendricks, we have the Leonards, we have so many names that have been there for years. And I'm not up here to battle. But it seems like right now we're putting North and South against each other again.

Historically, the intentional disruption of the African American family has been a primary tool of white supremacy,[12] one with deep roots extending from the time of chattel slavery (also evoked through Johnson's comment about "putting North and South against each other again," as in the Civil War) through the present era of mass incarceration. Further, such family disruption has often been cited as a reason African American students have historically faced academic failure. Perhaps most famously, in "The Negro Family: The Case For National Action," sociologist Daniel Patrick Moynihan wrote that "at the heart of the deterioration of the fabric of Negro society is the deterioration of the Negro family" and that "a prime index of the disadvantage of

Negro youth in the United States is their consistently poor performance on the mental tests that are a standard means of measuring ability and performance in the present generation."[13] What is not mentioned in this narrative, though, is the role that structural actors—policymakers, school officials, and others who make decisions on scales large and small—play in this disruption of family connections. Whether children were taken from their parents during slavery or parents were taken from their children by mass incarceration, black families in the United States have been forced to weather injustice after injustice, and as we saw in chapter 2, school systems can sometimes play a malignant role. Now, with an understanding of that history, the community members who speak during the hearings are asking those in power to take a different route—for once, to acknowledge a different truth about their schools, their communities, and their families. At Williams, one parent links the school closing to genocide. "My mother, my cousins, my grandmother went to Daniel Hale Williams," she says. "We have a long tradition at this school, and to rename it and to do all those others things is, it's a big . . . it's like you're killing our generation off."

Retired teacher and community member Simone Clark makes this connection between family disruption and the dismantling of African American community and social life even more explicit, while also mentioning its implications for Bronzeville and its historical significance as a center of black culture.

> You are destroying a family for many children who don't always have the easiest family situations in their homes. . . . A school is a community and a family and that is what is being destroyed here. Not only is it a family at the moment, but as you have heard people talk, and I was a history teacher for many years—this is a historical family. This is a family from one of the original and

important African American communities in the city of Chicago, and Mayo School represents the historical continuity of the Bronzeville community in an extraordinarily important way.

The concept Clark introduces here, the "historical family," is a way of binding together kinship ties and the historical significance of a place and its people to make a very different assessment of their worth than efficiency or value-added metrics.[14]

In the case of Williams, much of the challenge to the official district narrative relates to colocation with Urban Prep, an all-boys charter high school equally lauded for sending large numbers of its virtually all-black student body to college each year and criticized for pushing out students whose academic problems are deemed too challenging.[15] Teacher Nakia Mosby, who earlier questioned the district's reliance on a single year of test scores, pointed out that in calculating available "underutilized" building space, Williams was being penalized for resources and spaces that its students were not actually able to use.

> Just as a point of clarification, where it says that Drake will be relocating to the Williams Elementary and Middle building which will offer—the third bullet point—"a building that has received 6.8 million in recent facility investment." Williams Middle did not benefit from that investment. That investment was strictly for Urban Prep. Everything that was done as far as ADA accessibility and other upgrades, that was for the high school. We have no access to that entry, we have no access to the third floor and the portion of the building that was—that those upgrades you know has been received. We do not have elevators. The high school has that. They utilize that. Those upgrades was strictly for Urban Prep and not for us. So that's misleading right there, that information.

This comment introduces an element of tension that was an undercurrent to many conversations about school closures in 2013: that while CPS claimed to have too many empty buildings and not enough students, the district had quite recently added new charter schools to its "portfolio." In 2004, CPS launched an initiative it called Renaissance 2010, a pledge to shut down failing schools and open one hundred new schools.[16] Renaissance 2010 was announced at the Commercial Club of Chicago, which comprises leaders from top corporations in the region, and business leaders lauded the move—especially because two-thirds of the schools would be charter or contract schools. Critics questioned whether there were enough high-quality teachers and principals in the city to support so many new schools. Now, less than a decade later, many neighborhood schools were stung by the suggestion that CPS somehow had too many schools so shortly after a flurry of opening new ones. As Mosby's comments showed, being held accountable for "investment" that had benefited only the neighboring charter school added insult to injury.

Parent Evelyn Scott, unable to attend the Williams meeting, sent a friend to read a letter in her stead. She challenged the narrative that Drake was a better school than Williams and questioned the decision-making process, which she considered to be a farce. She addressed her letter "to Barbara Byrd-Bennett, or whoever is seeking to undermine my intelligence":

> It burns me up inside to hear that you have decided to close down my children's school due to underenrollment or lack of performance only to replace their school with a school which is pretty much identical. It's an outrage and not a good choice. Though I am not a rocket scientist, I am wise enough to see that no serious thought was put into place by your staff when the decision

> was made for the improvement of my children's education. . . . If you were aware of the fact that we were not utilizing the space to its full potential, why didn't anyone from downtown come into Williams to offer their services to assist us?

"Why didn't anyone from downtown come into Williams to offer their services to assist us?" Here Scott points out something that seems excruciatingly obvious yet has gone undiscussed in the official district narrative: Where is the accountability from district leaders themselves? Her question reminds us of Byrd-Bennett's damning comment that the schools slated for closure are "underresourced." Is it fair for those charged with allocating resources to levy that accusation against those who are supposed to receive them? And why are the officials presenting the data portraying the closing and receiving schools as drastically different when they are not?

Chicago Teachers Union representative Wallace Newkirk also directly countered Byrd-Bennett's narrative that the closings were neutral and not racist. On the contrary, he argued, the decision to close the schools was based on a desire to systematically disempower black and Latino communities, and the performance criteria were intended only to justify the decision ex post facto.

> For too long CPS—and I want this on the record—for too long CPS and the Board of Education have claimed that they could improve our schools by closing them. School closings, turnarounds, and privatizations have targeted African American and Latino neighborhoods for years. I mean, where are—and I'm not casting aspersions—but where are the white community schools in this room or at any of these hearings? They're all African American. And you gotta think about that. . . . [CPS and the

> board] have targeted African American and Latino neighborhoods for years. Latino schools as well. The voices of our communities have been ignored as we have demanded an end to school actions that destabilize our neighborhoods, take resources from our students, and increase racial inequities in Chicago.[17]

The quick aside with which Newkirk begins his statement—"I want this on the record"—is technically superfluous, since district officials opened the hearing by stating that a court reporter was present and that all comments would be recorded and conveyed to the CEO. By emphasizing that he wants his comment on the record, Newkirk reinforces the significance of what he is about to say while implying that the officials may not be taking notes as they said they would. Loretta Jeffries, a grandparent at the Overton hearing, makes a similar comment: "You know, y'all already planned to close Overton. I just want to know, because it's worrying me—is y'all's tapes and stuff on? Is y'all really documenting this?" Both Newkirk and Jeffries are concerned that CPS is playing what Jitu Brown referred to in chapter 1 as the "shell game"—that they will say one thing and do another, as they have done so many times.

Additionally, by stating, "they're all African American" and "you gotta think about that," Newkirk suggests that school closing proceedings should be judged not only by disparity in *intentions*, but by disparity in *outcome*; if the schools on the proposed list are all African American, that merits closer examination regardless of how they got on the list.

At the Overton meeting, parent Josita Curtis quoted Byrd-Bennett directly and, like Scott, questioned why those in charge of the system that created the present circumstances can't bear the consequences, which instead are directed toward students, teachers, and families.

> As I was reading this paper, and it stated something about "the reality is that too many of our children are being cheated out of a quality education they deserve because they are trapped in under-resourced and underutilized schools." . . . . Y'all talkin' about some repairs or "trapped." The only way they're trapped is because of the system, because they don't have a voice, and because everyone is looking upon a certain area, oh, because they [the schools] not full. I'm trying to keep my tears back 'cause we got kids back there looking at people that they not gon' see no more. . . . Y'all gonna tell them where they can and can't go? Y'all are a gang too!

In the context of a meeting where there is much discussion about gangs and violence (as I will discuss further below), Curtis's accusation rings sharply. Other participants suggested that the board and district officials are complicit in something profoundly immoral, saying things like, "I don't know how y'all can sleep at night" and calling the plan for closure "evil and devilish." But by calling them a *gang*, Curtis evoked something much harsher: a coordinated, collective attack inflicting terror on the community, and a cavalier act of violence with no regard for who is caught in the cross fire.

Whereas Brent and Meadows use causal language (e.g., "and thus") to argue that the schools slated for closure are not good schools based on the constructs of "performance" and efficiency, community members suggest other criteria for judging the schools: their history and their legacy as community anchors within Bronzeville. While these attributes could fairly be considered important to stakeholders of any school, they hold a particular symbolic weight given the historical significance of Bronzeville in the twentieth century. These divergent testimonies are more than just differences of opinion—they reflect different realities located on opposite sides of a racially and socioeconomically segregated world, shaped not only by different experiences but, in the case of the community members, by generations of knowledge and firsthand perspective.

In their testimonies before the hearing officer, multiple Mayo children referred to the school's upcoming fiftieth anniversary, suggesting that they understood the importance of some of the school's history that they had not themselves lived through. One third grader described how painful it was to find out about the proposed closure and how much "shame" it caused:

> My whole class started breaking out crying, so did my teacher. We walked through the halls in shame because we didn't want Mayo to close. When I'm in fourth grade, I was really thinking about going to the fiftieth year anniversary, but how can I when Mayo is closing?

Other students refer to the Mayo school song, which they view as an important tradition. A seventh grader speaks:

> Every day I go to school, we sing the Mayo song, and we are proud to hear the song. We are proud to sing the song every . . . every day. All I want to know is, why close Mayo? This is one of the best schools we ever had.

And another student:

> Just like everybody else was saying when they came up, what's the point of closing Mayo when it been on 37th Street for fifty whole years. And I have, like, I have a granny and she's like sixty-two right now . . . and she had went to Mayo. . . . And she like always tell me stories about, um, that the song that they'd be singing [begins to cry] that we sing still, that we still sing today.

For these students, singing the school song—a recognition of history and legacy—is itself a marker of goodness ("we are proud to hear the song . . . this is one of the best schools we ever had") as well as a representation of close family ties, something that spans generations. And at the end of the hearing, attendees begin to sing the Mayo school song.

At Williams, the proposed plan for closure dictated that Drake would move into the building occupied by Williams and the school's name would change to Drake—honoring John B. Drake, a white hotel magnate of the nineteenth century. Some community members were particularly offended by this proposition. The school had been named for Daniel Hale Williams, an African American doctor who performed the first open-heart surgery in the nation and founded Bronzeville's Provident Hospital, which served black patients at a time when many hospitals would not.[18] Thus changing the school's name was perceived as an affront not only to the school's legacy, but to the history of Bronzeville and of African American heroes in general. One speaker at the Williams hearing stated that it was "just a disrespect": "we went to *Daniel Hale Williams*, the first black open-heart surgeon, and that meant a lot. And it still means a lot."

In light of this concern, Brent's standard script regarding school performance was amended at the April 26 hearing for Williams, where he stated, "Finally, if the CEO's proposal is approved and the community later wishes to consider changing the school's name, the requirements of the board's school renaming policy will be followed to ensure both school and community engagement in evaluating potential new names." There is no justification for why the school cannot remain Williams. Today the school building occupies an odd middle ground: the metal sign outside proclaims in bold letters that the school is officially called Drake, while the original engraved stone above the door announces the name as Williams, and a metal plaque nearby honors Daniel Hale Williams as the school's namesake.

"YOU'RE PUTTING OUR CHILDREN'S LIVES ON THE LINE"

Many community members expressed concern for their children's security, citing tensions between closing schools and receiving schools and the difficulties of traveling a strange route to school. Parents' and teachers' concerns about students' safety are far from hypothetical. While gun violence in Chicago in general has received a great deal of local and national media attention in recent years, there is a particular linkage between the fear of school closure and the fear that children face death: the heartbreaking story of Derrion Albert, who was beaten to death in 2009 during a fight that many attributed to student conflict after a school closure and consolidation.[19] During the scripted portion of the hearing, district representatives promised that safety and security measures would be taken and that the Safe Passage program—where representatives from community organizations usher children to and from school—would be expanded. However, many parents and teachers had doubts, suggesting that Brent's assurances about the program were naive, ill-informed, or misguided. At the Williams meeting, teacher Jessica Wellington invoked the students themselves as experts on safety—experts no one had consulted:

> Now let's just be realistic here. You know there are boundaries, and some of my students had to tell me about them. If you ask them, they'll let you know which boundaries they cannot cross because they're going into this gang's territory and that gang's territory. What are we doing to make sure that they can actually walk to and from school? A situation happened at another school over by our area where that child got beat to death. How

> is CPS addressing that and [able to] confirm that that would never happen again? . . . What can we do for those students, how is that going to be addressed in writing to our parents and our community for their safe travels?

In noting that some of her students had to inform her about gang boundaries, Roberts admits that she does not share their expertise—meaning that representatives from the Office of Safety and Security are also likely to lack the information needed to keep their promises about students' safety. By noting that she wants to see the issue "addressed in writing," she implies that promises from the board cannot be accepted or believed unless they are recorded like a formal contract.

Phylicia Columbus, speaking at the Mayo meeting, frames her concerns about violence in a manner intended to invoke both empathy and a sense of justice.

> When you shut down the schools, now you're gonna send my special ed kid walking through a bad neighborhood by himself. Is that fair to him? When you close these schools, you're putting our children's lives on the line. Have some sympathy for us parents that have to work. I work at 147th and Halsted. My child goes to school at Mayo. If something happens with them walking to another school, is that fair for me to have to try to get from 147th and Halsted to see what's going on while he walking to school? Mayo did a lot for these children, and CPS is making very bad decisions right now, and somebody needs to stop it before we have more kids killed on the street.

Columbus's account, which focuses on her family's individual narrative (her son, her job, and their specific circumstances), stands in contrast to the district officials' language, which avoided naming any particular individuals or even referring to children more generally. By illustrating the specifics of her situation, Columbus reframes the dialogue from a large-scale view (the building, the classrooms, the test scores) to a focus on a single individual, her son: his circumstances, and what the district fairly owes him. She also brings to the fore the day-to-day reality of what it will mean for her, as a parent, to cope with the aftermath of his school's closing. In the eyes of the district, being relocated to a nearby "welcoming school" should mean an opportunity for a better education. For the Columbus family it means disruption of the services her child needs and the relationships he has formed as a student with a disability. It means potential threats to his safety. Working almost twenty miles from where her child currently goes to school, she experiences increased anxiety and uncertainty as he is moved to a new setting where neither he nor she has relationships with the adults around him.

More generally, community members cited past instances where trust had been violated as evidence that CPS's promises regarding safety or anything else could not be believed. Loretta Jeffries, the speaker at the Overton hearing who asked whether the event was actually being recorded, reminded attendees of the city's failed bid for the 2016 Olympics (with its proposal for an athletes' village in the Bronzeville area, along the lakefront) as evidence that the closure proposal had an ulterior motive.[20]

> Y'all want our building though. Yup. 'Cause the university want that land. Y'all don't know. . . . I'm the community person. I see what goes on in that neighborhood. Why we can't keep our school? There was a time when the Olympics was coming. Y'all remember they was gonna have the Olympics? They was gonna tear up all of King Drive. Well, since they lost the deal, they said, oh, we'll skip over to Overton. No! Leave our babies alone!

Much like the hunger strikers in chapter 1, Jeffries understands that what happens to Overton is not simply about Overton. The school is a bellwether for the community's future, and this latest threat against the school is only the most recent in a long line of assaults on its integrity and attempts to use it as a pawn in a broader plan for displacing residents of the South Side.

WHOSE REALITY COUNTS?

The students, parents, teachers, and community members who took time to appear at the hearings described in this chapter were doing more than arguing that their schools were "good schools" in the face of accusations of failure. They were arguing that their vision of the world, their experience, their very reality was valid. They had to make an argument for history: an argument that the events outlined in chapter 2 actually took place, an argument for considering the long-term impact of racism, and an argument that the legacy of each school actually counted for something. And they had to make an argument for the value of care and relationships: that the bonds shared within each school mattered, that they were tangible and irreplaceable. This version of reality—in which the value of a school is directly related to its nurture and support of lasting human relationships, and in which history matters—stood opposed to another reality. In this other reality, numbers don't lie, the question of "good school" versus "failing school" is simple and beyond debate, and the only history that matters is last year's test scores. And it is the second reality that comes with the power of enforcement. Hence, today Overton, Williams, and Mayo are all closed.

The district's version of reality, in which numbers allow for a final and indisputable call about a school's future, is not unique to Chicago or to this situation. It reflects the national policy trend

I discussed earlier in this chapter of attempting to quantify every aspect of the educational process. This in turn reflects the broader move toward neoliberalism in education. While neoliberalism is a broad idea that takes many forms in different contexts, in the context of public education it constitutes a set of ideals that assume that efficiency is an important goal in managing schools and public education systems; that the best way to achieve such efficiency is to allow schools to function within a free market system based on competition, where the best schools will succeed and the worst ones will be driven to improve or shut down; that private entities like for-profit companies and corporations should be allowed to participate freely in this marketplace and are better at delivering services than public entities such as the government; and that the success of individuals should also be allowed to play out within the free market, with the assumption that the most deserving will succeed by working hard and navigating the system.[21] Through a neoliberal lens, "rather than 'citizens,' with rights, we are consumers of services. People are 'empowered' by taking advantage of opportunities in the market."[22]

This set of assumptions fails to account for some basic realities in a public school system. First, any enterprise dealing with the care and nurturing of children is likely to be inefficient at times, and striving for efficiency often requires sacrificing things like care, patience, and flexibility. Second, although a marketplace is premised on "winners" and "losers" competing against each other, the "consumers" in this case (parents and children) are not operating on a level playing field. The children who enter a school system may face poverty, homelessness, hunger, and health issues, and they vary in identity—in race, gender, disability, language practices, and all the other things that make them who they are. Public schools have to account for all of these differences, which shape the outcomes they are measured on (graduation rates, standardized test scores, and so on). This leads us to the third problem: neoliberalism pushes schools to focus on the "winners," those exceptional students who will be successful by these limited metrics, and to abandon students who might lead to inefficiencies.

And so, through the logic of neoliberalism, we find ourselves observing the dual realities reflected in this chapter. We see schools that in many ways are nearly identical forced to compete against each other instead of uniting in their shared educational goals. We see them judged by how "efficient" they are and how effectively they meet quantifiable metrics, with district officials presenting a case that one school is better than another based on differences that statisticians would be hard-pressed to call significant. We see the reality of the students these schools serve—students facing challenges brought on by racism, multigenerational injustice, housing insecurity, and poverty—being ignored in a calculation of their future. We see a willful ignorance of a history of explicit racism and a failure to critically examine the extension of that history into the present. We see a system that fails to take responsibility for creating the conditions of that social instability, preferring to act as though it's all a matter of individuals' pulling themselves up by their bootstraps and teachers' needing to work harder.

It is impossible to get around the fact that the school closure process outlined in this chapter was racist. To many, this claim will seem too bold or impossible to prove—How can we know what was in the hearts and minds of those involved, since many if not all certainly care about children and desire racial equity? Remember, though, that the question of racism is not about intentions, it's about outcomes. In other words, student Jordan McKendrick had it right. "I feel like this is so racist of y'all to close down all these CPS schools," she said, "because most—you see, most black kids going to CPS schools." As community members understand, the school closings are racist because they have disparate impact and because they are rooted in a racist history in which institutional actors have demonstrated ill intent (as one Overton meeting participant put it, "turning Bronzeville into Rahmsville," implying that the mayor had authoritarian intentions for the community), unreliability, or at best ignorance about how to ensure the safety and sustainability of the community. And so, when people stand up and argue for their schools, they are not only arguing to keep one building open. As with the fight for Dyett, these school battles are about much more than individual sites. Community members are fighting for an acknowledgment of past harms, an honest reckoning of present injustice, and an acceptance of their reality—a reality in which a school's value is about much more than numbers.

These two realities are at odds, and they don't exist in a vacuum. One group—CPS officials—has more power to ensure that decisions are based on their operating reality. So the discrepancy is not settled through logic, or debate, or internal validity, or the will of the majority. The "enrollment efficiency range," for instance, is not clearly motivated by any facet of child development research, professional expertise, or any other transparent factors. It includes figures that seem peculiarly arbitrary to carry so much weight (e.g., the notion that "76 to 77 percent" of a building's classrooms should be occupied). But because of the balance of power, the claims emerging from the school district win the day. Therefore Overton, Williams, and Mayo all are closed now, and it seems that no amount of tears or pleading, logic or history, could have saved them.

4 *Mourning*

For long years we of the world gone wild have looked into the face of death and smiled.
—W. E. B. Du Bois, *Darkwater*

On the one hand, there is the loss of place and the loss of time, a loss that cannot be recovered or recuperated but that leaves its enigmatic trace. And then there is something else that one cannot "get over," one cannot "work through," which is the deliberate act of violence against a collectivity, humans who have been rendered anonymous for violence and whose death recapitulates an anonymity for memory.
—Judith Butler, "After Loss, What Then?"

I'm eighteen. I play pick-up basketball games with ghosts.
—Nate Marshall and Demetrius Amparan, "Lost Count: A Love Story"

DEATH BY ANOTHER NAME: LOVE, LOSS, AND INSTITUTIONAL MOURNING

I believe in ghosts.

I haven't always. I remember the day: I was cleaning my classroom after school, when Ms. Samuels walked in. She was a paraprofessional who also ran a popular girls' mentoring program and was known for her sense of humor, her candor, and the personal attention with which she cared for the children at our school—alternating between warmth and sometimes strict words.

"You know," she told me offhandedly, "I went to this school. Right here in this building. It used to be Douglas." I knew that one of the stones on the building's exterior was carved with "Douglas," but I'd never thought to ask why. She told me how as a teenager she had frequently cut class and been caught up with trouble. Now, as she found herself employed in the very building where she'd gotten into fights and ignored her teachers, she considered it a sign. God was giving her a second chance—the opportunity to nurture young people needing guidance as she had once needed it. And what about Douglas, I asked? Closed, she explained. Closed when they tore down the projects.

That's when I first started seeing ghosts.[1] Not exciting ghosts—no literal apparitions, no translucent beings floating down the hallway. It was just a nagging presence, a thought as fleeting as it was sudden. *There were so many other children here*. I would see them in the auditorium—running where they weren't supposed to run, cracking jokes, resisting teachers trying to get them to hush, pulling each other aside to share a bag of chips or a whispered secret. I'd never known them, but that didn't change their having been there.

For me, of course, these ghosts weren't real memories. But for many black Chicagoans the ghosts are present in everyday life. "'I always think of double Dutch," said a woman sitting outside Dyett one day while it was still closed. "The whole line of girls playing double Dutch, all along this way. And I used to enter through that door."[2] These ghosts are stewards of lives marked by mourning: mourning those lost to the many forms of violence this country has invented to kill us. We mourn those killed by police; we mourn those killed directly or indirectly by the violence of hunger and desperation or the violence of poverty and poor health; we mourn those taken from us and imprisoned. And, as I will argue, we mourn those institutions, like our schools, that have helped shape our sense of who we are.

Institutional mourning is the social and emotional experience undergone by individuals and communities facing the loss of a shared institution they are affiliated with—such as a school, church, residence, neighborhood, or business district—especially when those individuals or communities occupy a socially marginalized status that amplifies their reliance on the institution or its significance in their lives. Although institutional mourning can occur in many contexts, here I explore its traits within the context of school closure and examine what this "death" means for the African American community of Bronzeville. Of course, we have already seen the metaphor of death used to talk about Chicago's school closures. "It's like you're killing our generation off [by closing the school]," said one Williams Elementary parent. "This is not rhetoric. They killed this school," says Jitu Brown when discussing Dyett. As we have seen in the previous chapters, a school closing is much more than the loss of an interchangeable building. It can be a harbinger of things to come, the culmination of multiple generations of racism and injustice and a blatant disregard of the fundamental reality within which a community understands itself. A school closure can thus be a devastating event that leaves an indelible emotional aftermath. In this chapter, we will look at institutional mourning to better understand why people fight so fiercely for their schools even when others have labeled them a failure. They fight because losing them can mean losing their very world.

BLACK INSTITUTIONS AND BLACK MOURNING

For human beings, an attachment to "home" or a sense of place is perhaps universal, but it manifests itself differently across time, geography, and subculture. (Consider, for instance, how the meaning of "home" may differ for a twentieth-century nomadic herder in Morocco and a nineteenth-century traveler crossing the Rocky Mountains. For African American city dwellers, who continue to live the legacy of Jim Crow, "home" often includes an attachment to certain institutions.[3]

Segregation in American cities, although it has declined since 1970, remains high. At the current rate of decline, it would take 150 years for black-white segregation to reach low levels.[4] Such segregation has contributed to what sociologist William Julius Wilson calls social isolation,[5] creating closed social networks that have limited overlap with the institutions of dominant white society. While Wilson's theory refers specifically to poor black city dwellers, middle-class or affluent black Americans may retain attachments to many of the same institutions as poor African Americans, whether through utility (going to a hair salon that serves black clientele), through emotional bonds (attending the same church as one's parents or other relatives), or because most middle-class and even relatively affluent African Americans in the United States still live in neighborhoods that are majority black.[6]

Perhaps as a by-product of segregation and its legacy, African Americans as a group have a political sensibility that is less individualistic than the American mainstream. Within black communities, there is a focus on uplifting the collective and "giving back to the community" as opposed to viewing success only in terms of private property and individual triumphs. As political scientist Michael Dawson describes it, this ideology dates back to Reconstruction. For many black people "the advancement of the self, the liberation of the self, is a meaningless concept outside the context of one's community."[7]

The continued wealth gap between black and white Americans may also play a role. In 2013 the net worth of white households was thirteen times that of black households—an increase since

1983, when white households had eight times as much wealth.[8] This gap may encourage African Americans to rely on shared institutions and resources to compensate for diminished individual resources. For instance, black people donate 25 percent more of their discretionary income to charitable causes than their white peers do and are far more likely to give to churches—with the understanding that as their contributions support those in need, they may one day be supported.[9]

Some scholars have described this bond between black families and their churches as paralleled by their bond with their schools. These bonds are defined by a sense of shared participation and ownership—a sense that *this place is ours*.[10] In many places, as black people arrived during the Great Migration, these bonds created cities within cities: the black Seventh Ward in Philadelphia, Bronzeville in Chicago, Harlem in New York City, and so on.[11] On this smaller scale, the institutions one encounters in everyday life take on grander significance. Structures like the Supreme Life Building at 35th and King Drive (home of the North's first black-owned insurance company) or the Pilgrim Baptist Church at 33rd and Indiana (the birthplace of modern gospel music) take on the importance of the World Trade Center or the National Cathedral—cultural icons looming large not only in the imagination but in daily life.

Even African American mourning practices reflect communal bonds. In a survey of about fifteen hundred grieving individuals, psychologists have found that compared with white people, African Americans maintain a stronger sense of continuing bonds with the deceased after death. This trend diverges from the dominant way we think of grief in a society that promotes the importance of "moving on" by severing these bonds.[12] African Americans are more likely to grieve the loss of extended family members beyond the nuclear unit.[13] Black mourners also are more likely to experience *complicated grief*, a prolonged form characterized by symptoms such as unbidden memories or intrusive fantasies of the lost relationship, strong spells or pangs of emotion related to the lost relationship, and a loss of interest in social activities.[14]

These same "symptoms," or aspects of mourning—a sense that bonds continue after death and grief persisting long after loss (in this case, two years)—were present in the stories of Bronzeville residents I spoke to. Parents, teachers, students, and community members—each affiliated with a closed school—described these institutional attachments in their own words. "In essence, you know how your school, your church, that's the place, that's what makes it your home. I still see those folks coming back to the Robert Taylor Homes and sitting out there in that grassy area with their lawn chairs," said Sharon Munro,[15] a teacher who had experienced two consecutive school closures. Munro is referring to the practice, described by sociologist Mary Pattillo,[16] of former Bronzeville public housing residents' demonstrating loyalty and commitment to the projects they once lived in, even after they have been demolished, by holding regular picnics where they stood.

Odetta McNealy, a Bronzeville resident who sent several children, grandchildren, and foster children to the same school before it closed, describes some residents' reliance on schools for social support as a matter of personal strength and resources—those who don't have them draw on the institution for support. "Everyone is not strong like some of us are," she says. "And everyone has their separate issues. The schools were like second homes for some people, and there were resources out there for children who didn't have that safe haven at home."

"WE'RE ALL IN IT TOGETHER": STORIES OF LOVE

When we remember what we've lost, we remember first with love. In institutional mourning this doesn't just mean love for a school or for the people in it. It can also mean love for *ourselves* within the school. In losing a school one loses a version of oneself—a self understood to be a member of a community, living and learning in relation to other community members. Without the school to act as a hub, that membership is gone.[17] "At [my closed school], I never felt vulnerable," says teacher Katherine Warner. "I felt safe and strong. And then they closed it." We can think of this form of love as a logical extension of the southern African philosophy of *ubuntu*, frequently translated as "I am because you are" or, as Archbishop Desmond Tutu has explained the concept, "my humanity is inextricably bound up in yours." If I am because you are, it follows that my understanding of myself is bound up in my relation to you and my place within our network of relationships. When the school dies, a version of the self dies with it.

Teacher Lynn Ross describes how her school was characterized by love between teachers and students, defining it as a relationship of protection. "We had that mind-set of *those are our babies*," she says emphatically. "Those were *our* babies. We gon' talk about 'em, but you better not! We will fuss at them. We fussed at 'em all the time. But don't treat our babies unfairly. You will not. No."[18] Martin, a former student at two schools that are now closed, says of his grammar school, "I loved being there. . . . We had computer lab and we had after-school programs and stuff like that. It was, it was just—I liked being there." Recalling his high school experience, he, like Ross, invokes the language of a family, where interpersonal conflicts or challenges are superseded by bonds. "We had teachers there that was like family. . . . At the end of the day we were family. We made sure that we was together. Because we argued, but we were still family and we were still together."

Warner, the teacher who explained how she "felt safe" at her school, described her love in terms of both such family bonds and her own sense of personal and professional development, particularly as a white teacher in a school with mostly black faculty and virtually all black students. “I was the Emerson cheerleader. I loved Emerson. . . . I was one of the people who brought in the restorative justice program. And people came from all over. Not just Chicago—we had a whole group from Wisconsin to observe our program. It was fun, and interesting. . . . [My colleagues and the students] were always teaching me things. [I enjoyed] being able to talk about stuff. Being able to talk about racism and prejudice and creating that environment where they’re really fascinated by having that conversation was wonderful. I loved it.” Warner described staying after hours to work on projects with colleagues and enthusiastically attending extracurricular and sporting events. She contrasted that level of involvement with her current teaching position at an elite school on the North Side, with far more material resources at her disposal. “[At Emerson] it was very much a home-community situation. Which was great. It was really great. [Now] I’m doing the best teaching I’ve ever done, because it’s all I’m doing. But I’m not enjoying it the way I enjoyed being an integral part of a community, which I think is what neighborhood schools have to be in order to survive and function. This idea that everybody there is just an integral part of this mission. You’re in it together. And even if it’s bad, it’s okay because we’re all in it together and we’ve got our arms linked.” Although Warner’s new school offers conditions that should make for a rewarding teaching experience, she said she misses the sense of self she cultivated at the old school, which she can’t recover. In a sense, some of this sense of self was developed in the context of the precarious situation; when she was teaching where nothing was certain (CPS policy, safety, the future of the neighborhood), Warner nevertheless was comforted by the idea that she and everyone else in her school could face the future together.

McNealy, the parent, grandparent, and foster parent, described a similar sense of shared mission at her family’s closed school, which had housed a child-parent center where teachers collaborated in teams with a community representative to provide comprehensive resources for parents. “It was a circle of love,” she said, describing the activities her children did at school, which she felt enhanced their self-love as African Americans, such as memorizing poems like “Hey, Black Child” by Bronzeville poet Useni Eugene Perkins and “Still I Rise” by Maya Angelou. “They were happy,” she said of her children and the others she worked with at the center. “They knew they were loved. They wanted to be there. We [parents] wanted to be there.”

Teacher Amanda Moss, who experienced three school closings in a row (two in Bronzeville), described a similar nurturing of personal and professional development. Her first job was at a school she knew would be closing, and she was hired only to complete the year, which allowed her to maintain a degree of emotional detachment. However, at her second school she settled in comfortably for seven years before its closing was announced. She was animated in recounting the experience of developing curricula and activities in her field of English literature and described the satisfaction of seeing students thrive:

> And I mean, that's where I got really invested. You know? I mean, I really learned to teach there. . . . And I got to be the AP [advanced placement] English teacher! And I was so excited and I just—Because you could totally make your own curriculum. And I got to do that. And I, you know, I *loved* that class. . . . I had some students who participated with me in that CPS Shakespeare [program with the Chicago Shakespeare Theater]. It was a beautiful experience . . . and I mean they just, they so shined. I mean they were so involved, so dedicated, you know to this experience. It was awesome. So I loved Burleigh High School.

In the public narrative about closed schools, these are stories we rarely hear. Using words like love in a conversation about educational policy decisions feels almost taboo, or somehow in poor taste. Perhaps it's rude to talk about love in polite company. Instead, closing schools are presented as uniformly valueless, without worth, and characterized mostly by criteria that are as far as you can get from something as base and as messy as human emotion. How many students can the building hold? How much will it cost to repair it? What test scores did it have last year? But for those closest to these schools, these questions swim beneath the surface of something much more important: love.

DEFENDING THE DEAD

Each of these Bronzeville school closures took place within the cloud of a narrative of the school's failure as an institution—from Barbara Byrd-Bennett's description of children "cheated" out of an education because they were "trapped," to the quantitative comparisons between schools at closure hearings, to the language of Dyett as "chronically underperforming." Community members were keenly aware of this narrative and its implications—that in naming the school as a failure, public discourse also implicated *them* as failures as students, parents, and teachers. Much like a relative tasked with eulogizing someone who was imperfect, perhaps even deeply flawed, but nevertheless loved, they flinched under the weight of these public characterizations and spoke both candidly and protectively about the lost institution. Like a person, the school does not have to be perfect to be mourned; it can be acknowledged as flawed, but its death is no less unjust.

"I felt bad," said one student, Chanelle, "because I felt like Emerson is actually a good school! Emerson is not what people make it seem. People make it seem like it's just a horrible place." Martin used similar language to describe his closed high school. "The thing about [it] is when you're in that school—when you're *in* the school, though, it's like, it's not what they try to make it look."

Amanda Moss, the AP English teacher, responded specifically to the rhetoric of "failure" that surrounds school closure: "I never considered us a failing school or failing teachers or failing students. I felt like pretty much everyone in that building was working really hard for those kids, whether it was at Emerson or at Burleigh. Trying to push them forward as far as they could go. You know, you meet the students where they are, not where you would ideally want them to be. . . . And you keep pushing. . . . And it's possible." Here Moss insisted on the school as a site not of failure, but of perseverance and growth, despite external language of failure and the real complications of student and teacher limitations.

Psychologist Paul C. Rosenblatt and chaplain Beverly Wallace, in *African-American Grief*, found that bereaved interviewees spoke of the ongoing pain of not being able to access the bonds once shared with the lost person. One participant described grieving as "a mourning and a sorrowfulness [about] . . . having [lost] physical access to engage in dialogue and to recall memories and to use as a resource for guidance, and so that is no longer there, as being able to call them up on the phone, to stop in to their house, because it's not available to us in this realm that we live in, so that's the sorrowful part."[19] Their findings are echoed in a story Martin told me about frequently walking past Gridley Elementary on his way to work. The building doesn't house a new school but simply sits dark. He vividly described the emotions and memories that rise as he passes.

> Because sometimes when I walk [by] I do feel disappointed and sad because when I go to [work] I cut through my old school all the time. . . . And as a kid that's the same walk I made going to

school every day. And it's just like, you just remember everything, like, you remember—I don't know if you feel that way?

[Ewing: Yeah.]

You remember a tree! We played near that tree and my brother would take us to school. . . . Like you'll walk to school with your brother and I see the tree and I see the school . . . and then I walk into my school. So it's like I would take a left and you would walk down and you just start remembering everything. Because like, it's this house, it's a house that you always remembered. . . . I remember I walked past it and I remember they were building it. Then I walked past this tree and there was a beehive there. And you know we were kids so—

[Ewing (laughs): You're throwin' . . .]

You're messing with the bees [laughs]. I know it's not good now, but you're messing with the bees and we're running from the bees and every time I walk past that tree I just think about the bees. When I walk past that house, I think about when they was building that house. And then you make it to the corner . . . and then like it's different memories everywhere you go. You make it to this corner and you look down this way and you look down that way. And down this way is where you walked into the alley when you was in seventh grade. . . . And I just remember how a bus used to sit in front of the school. . . . And then you just remember how when school had end-of-the-school-year bashes . . . how people who graduated would come back, and then you're like "Who was that?" . . . but he's cool because he's older. And you go through all that. And you just get a little bit angry because they use the school for different stuff now. And it's like you just see that. You just. . . . We got a field right there—I think I even remember when they was building that field. Wow. . . . And this is behind the school and then we used to play football there every morning. . . . And when I walk in there I just remember, this is on my journey to [work], I just remember, like, we played football there. And I get a little bit angry 'cause now you'll just see cars parked. . . . You just get a little bit angry because [of] all the memories and stuff.

In this extended narrative, Martin described, with great specificity, the quotidian details of his life at the now-closed school: a specific tree where he played, the childhood misdeed of disturbing a beehive, seeing older graduates of his school and looking up to them, playing football, walking with his brother. He spoke fluidly, the memories coming one after another, punctuated by descriptions of how he felt (disappointed, sad, angry). He periodically invited me into his memories—invited me to see his ghosts. At the beginning of the narrative he seemed concerned that what he was about to say might make me uncomfortable, and he checked for my affirmation ("I don't know if you feel that way?") before continuing. He told me he hesitates to share these feelings with others but at first has a hard time articulating precisely why.

I don't know how to say it though. But it's not something—it's kind of embarrassing sometimes. And it's not embarrassing as "oh, you're embarrassing, this is stupid." It's embarrassing as I don't know how to . . . it's like you have to talk about it and people are like—I don't know. I don't know how to say it, but I don't find myself talking about it a lot.

[Ewing: Do you feel like people will look at you a certain way?]

A certain—I don't even know how to say it but it's like not something you want to talk about a lot. It's not easy to talk about . . . it's not something that you just bring up. Because like I said it's not normal. It's not something that everybody has gone through. Sometimes when stuff is different it's like—oh, put it like [this]: You came to school with a mark on your face, right?

> And maybe it was a mark because you was doing something stupid and then people are intensely asking you questions.

Shame is a pervasive but rarely discussed aspect of the grieving experience. Grief can induce feelings of shame through many routes: shame at the stigma of death, shame at one's rage or anger, shame at one's own fear of death, shame at feeling weak or like a failure.[20] In this case Martin described not wanting to share his experience because others might find it aberrant or strange—"not normal." He compared it to coming to school with a mark on your face; since teachers are mandated reporters, CPS requires them to immediately call the Department of Children and Family Services. Thus the "mark" is like a scarlet letter: not only is it ugly and disfiguring, it prompts uncomfortable personal questions about one's home life and therefore one's own value as a person and the value of one's family. Given the rhetoric of school failure discussed above, Martin had reasonable fears that a frank conversation about school closure might bring similarly invasive and judgmental questions and personal assessments. What kind of person goes to a failing school?

COPING IN THE FACE OF VIOLENCE AND TRAUMA

Teachers also recalled the intense emotions they felt on learning that their schools would close. Munro called it "an amazing shock to the system."[21] Teacher Carlina Baker explained:

> Everybody was scared. You know, scared shitless basically . . . everybody was really scared. Everybody went to all the meetings, and we wrote speeches and got our best and brightest up there and said, "speak for Harding." And when I realized how the meetings were going it was like, Why waste your time? You

> know? It was like a slap in the face. And I still get like a little emotional about it just because [long pause] just because of like—of how *voiceless* we all felt. Yeah. So it was really hard. And at the end everybody kind of said, "Okay, we know this school is going to close, and we'll probably be moved somewhere else." That was the consensus that we were kind of—the reality, I guess, of it. Now my son's school closed as well.

In this account Baker described a cycle of feelings that preceded the actual loss of the school: fear surrounding the process, followed by collective efforts to fight the closing, then the startling realization that their efforts wouldn't succeed ("like a slap in the face"), followed by feelings of futility or voicelessness and then resignation, coupled with the unsettling news that her son's school, also in Bronzeville, would be closing as well. Baker, who in addition to being a classroom teacher is trained as an art therapist, used this perspective to draw direct connections between losing a school and grieving a death: "You go through a mourning period. Definitely. It's like a loss. And you're constantly reminded by this empty, this empty building that you still have to pass every day. Like a tombstone. You know it's just still sitting there, so yeah it's sad [small laugh]. It really is sad." Like Martin, Baker found her emotions triggered by passing the shuttered school as she went about her business in the neighborhood. Also like Martin, she responded to the perceived social taboo of talking about the death of the school, laughing with a slight awkwardness or embarrassment in the middle of her account as though to lessen any discomfort I might feel at her honest discussion of her own sadness.

Warner called the experience of closure "so demoralizing." She drew a parallel between the closure and student deaths that occurred at roughly the same time. "It was just—it was really bad. And that last year, in the last eight weeks of school, we lost three kids to violence. And then they closed my school." Warner went from the closed school to another school, where she felt deeply unhappy, before moving to her present position at the North Side school. In her new position she experienced such severe anxiety that she was hospitalized. In the two years between the school closure and the time of our interview, she theoretically should have had time to forge new bonds and move on professionally and personally. However, she said, "I don't know if I'll ever recover from losing that school." Like Martin, the teachers I interviewed also feared being considered "failures": they felt that being attached to a closing school was a scarlet letter and that they would be marked as bad teachers and would have a hard time finding new employment.

Other teachers described how their own emotional responses were compounded and amplified by an overall climate of stress, anxiety, and sadness as students and teachers struggled to cope with loss. Moss said she felt "devastated" and that everyone was "feed[ing] off of the same energy" to create a pervasive sense of stress and despair. "We were all depressed," she said. "I remember I started having panic attacks. So many people were just under so much stress. And the kids were very anxious. They didn't know what was going to happen to them."

McNealy described similar feelings of despair and hopelessness, and she was angry with the board of education for subjecting the community to these experiences. Like Baker, she described a moment of resigned certainty when she understood that attempts to save the school would be futile, and she called the hurtful decisions "intentional, premeditated to destroy."

> I sat right there on the corner . . . and I cried my eyes out. Do you know how it feels for me as a mama? I have raised my kids and

> my grandkids. And for them to do them like that—you can hurt me. I really don't care. But you don't have to hurt the babies. You don't. This is a hate crime. I said, "I don't care what you say. Y'all talkin' about kids." Look. . . . That hurt. Ain't no mama gonna let you hurt their kids. . . . So I knew then that it was a formula of destruction.

McNealy described this hurt as continuing long after students were supposed to be comfortably settled in receiving schools. She told of finding an eighth grader she knew breaking down in tears on her walk to her new school. "She said she hated school. [She] ain't never hated school! She grew up there. . . . They have broken, they have knocked the life out of many of these children. They have made them so unhappy. But besides that, they have hurt them. They have hurt them to no end."

Baker, speaking from the perspective of being an art therapist as well as a teacher, used the language of trauma to describe students' and teachers' attempts to cope with the closing, suggesting that the decision makers behind school closure needed to be more aware of its effects. "I have to say that Rahm Emanuel has to understand that it's a violent act against a community when you constantly do these type of things. And so there's definitely a PTSD [posttraumatic stress disorder] response. Even for the teachers, they're like 'Are you going to leave us too?' [when they are] talking to the principal." She mentioned public housing reunions to demonstrate that people in Bronzeville retain institutional bonds long after the institution itself has ceased to exist. "Even with the closing of the projects," she said, "Stateway Gardens, they have a big reunion every year where people come to Dunbar Park and meet up. It's like a humongous event. So it's like . . . yeah, you're losing your family." This connection between schools and housing reflects the community's particular history, discussed in chapter 2. For Bronzeville residents, these latest losses are not only about a single school or a single moment. They are echoes of something deeper, a sadness that precedes them and may outlive them. In experiencing a school closure, community members have to contend with a new shock to the system, but at the same time they may also be prompted to face unresolved traumas that are still raw and painful.

Understanding a death as occurring within the shadow of a larger act of injustice renders mourning at once personal and historical. While death is of course a natural part of the world we live in, deaths that feel unjust, and thereby unnatural, can leave us with unease that is hard to handle. Death that results from extreme violence, especially state violence, can feel anything but natural. As novelist and critic R. Clifton Spargo wrote, "Mourning a figure of the past [has] everything to do with the injustice of the present."[22] Spargo's words are part of an analysis of the works of the Jewish philosopher Emmanuel Levinas, who was a prisoner of war during World War II. Spargo writes that Levinas's work centers on "the historical specter of the unjust death." For Levinas, the long shadow of the Holocaust and the injustice of the world that produced it shapes the recollection of an individual person's death. The unjust death leaves us with a specter—an unsettled ghost, a phantom that is hard to shake off. For bereaved people, a critical part of mourning is trying to construct a narrative of someone's death as meaningful, or not. We hear this language all the time when someone's death is described as "honorable" or "senseless." In *African American Grief*, Paul Rosenblatt and Beverly Wallace describe how, for African American mourners, the experience of making meaning can be influenced by whether racism was directly or indirectly responsible for the loss.

> When economic discrimination or direct racism seems to a grieving African American to be partly or fully responsible for

a death, it may add elements of anger, rage, and indignation to the grief. . . . There are also matters of meaning making. People make meanings about the death as a part of the grief process. In making meaning, they come to a story about the person who died, what happened that brought about the death, and what feelings are appropriate.[23]

As I spoke to people mourning their schools, their stories were rife with adamant criticism of the way their schools were lost. Their belief that the process was fundamentally unjust shaped their grief. That is, seeing the death of the institution as unjust made them sadder or angrier, or it made it recovery harder. Asif Wilson, a teacher who joined the Dyett hunger strike in solidarity after the closure of his own school on the West Side, described being struck simultaneously by intense emotions and by a sense of the injustice of the closing.

I was on my couch when we heard about my school closing on [the local affiliate of] Fox News. They put a picture—they did their nine o'clock news broadcast from the front of [my school]. Like, "We're standing in front of [this school], one of the fifty schools that will be closed," and I'm like . . . [exhales] *Oh*. It goes to show the level of fucking disrespect these people have—I'll define it for you specifically: the board of education, the fucking mayor—for black communities. They didn't even have the compassion or care to tell the community before they told Fox News. They didn't send a memo out, they didn't send an email. You could have sent an official letter out to the families. You could have done a lot. But you only engage through a press release. They're fucking cowards. They're cowards. . . . I started crying. It was a really emotional time for all of us at the school. Because it was like . . . it was such an uninformed process. It was like, a hundred schools today. Fifty schools. And CPS—they'll do this! Sit,

> sit, sit. Hit real hard. Sit in our fucking closet, plan, be decisive, be very strategic in private. Which shows their lack of public accountability. They are not a transparent organization.

Wilson's story reflects the mistrust of CPS we have heard throughout this volume—a mistrust that has been earned over such a long period, through so much action and inaction, that it is hard to shake off. Prentice, a former student at a closed school, also blamed Mayor Rahm Emanuel for not being present or transparent about the school closure process, saying that if he were mayor he would personally visit schools before closing them. "If you're a boss, or if you're the mayor or whatever your position is, you shouldn't be scared to go out to the public. . . . A lot of them [who work at central office] are scared. You don't see them making any type of appearances in public. You know they're doing something secret. They're grimy. He's scary."

James Roberts, a parent and local business owner who was born in Bronzeville and is now raising his three children in the area, was even more straightforward. He called the public closure hearings "all bullshit. Public hearings are just there to let you talk. 'We already know what we're gonna do, but we're giving you a chance to feel good about talking.'" He echoed Prentice's point about district employees' failure to engage with the community, saying, "Some of them live in the suburbs. Some of them live in [white communities on the North Side such as] Lake View, Lincoln Park. And they don't leave that office. They don't go to any meetings in the community. They don't know and they really don't want to know."

Other participants shared Wilson's sense that the school closings were being part of a broader pattern of disrespect for people of color in Chicago, particularly black Chicagoans—to use McNealy's, term, a "formula of destruction." Martin, the student who spoke so vividly about his memories of playing football at his school, referred to the symbolic importance of the closed schools' names as evidence of this.

> When you take over, when you take over a 'hood—because the people that lived [the history] aren't going to live forever. The people that actually experienced, that lived that. And as you're getting older and you're listening to these stories at some point you still gotta move on and you can't—you're not going to remember everything your parents told you. So that's how you get black history to go away. That's how you get black history to go away. Closing schools. The schools I went to . . . [lists Bronzeville schools named for famous African Americans]. They're closing these schools down. That's how you get black history to go away. . . . It's like we've been through a lot and people always try to—I mean the same people who will take everything you have will blame it on you for not having anything.

That's how you get black history to go away. For Martin, losing a school is losing a piece of a history, a piece of self-understanding and personal narrative. As he sees it, the city is counting on those older black Chicagoans who carry this history to eventually disappear, and by shutting down the institutions that bear our collective memory, those in power ensure that it will be gone forever. In chapters 1 and 3 we heard residents stand up for the memories of Walter H. Dyett and Daniel Hale Williams as they fought to keep their schools' names. In many areas of the city where charter schools or other schools have occupied the buildings where older schools once stood, the names of black historical icons have already been wiped out. Mary C. Terrell Elementary—named for a black suffragist who was a charter member of the NAACP—became ACE Technical Charter School in 2001. Two years later,

Sojourner Truth Elementary School became the Chicago International Charter School. Ralph J. Bunche Elementary School, honoring the first African American to win a Nobel Prize, is now Providence Englewood Charter School.[24] Baker, the teacher and art therapist, concurred, arguing that to change the names of schools is "almost like they're erasing history." Like other teachers I spoke with, she challenged the narrative of the "failing school," but she tied her critique directly to racism and white supremacy. "The idea of closing a school based on test scores is just, it's so absurd to me. Especially with the standardized test scores and how they are, how they are centered in eugenics. . . . So you're closing schools in these areas that have been, like, harmed by institutionalized racism and white supremacy. You're closing these schools, these institutions that are pillars and blaming them."

Ross echoed this sense of being not only angry at the outcome of school closure, but upset about the means through which it was done. As a social studies teacher, she believed she was sensitive to and understanding of concepts like supply and demand and the economic constraints of a district budget, but she felt insulted at the hypocrisy with which the district deployed these concepts.

> What pissed me off so much was. . . . I mean, I *get* economics. . . . So some schools have to close. I absolutely get that. But you can't tell me that you don't have money, and in the same breath open charter schools. . . . I was aware of what was happening in the neighborhood and understood, because I'm a social science teacher, that it was because of gentrification. I don't even think that there was a real attempt to cover up the fact that . . . I mean, maybe they thought it was, because they just thought we're so ignorant. But I just thought, this is so *blatant*. And it started with the closing of King High School. It's almost like, "I poured gasoline on your house, and then it's your fault that it's on fire."

The metaphor Ross used here—pouring gasoline on your house, then blaming you for the fire—harks back to Martin's comment. "People will take everything you have, then blame you for having nothing." In both cases their observations seem to speak to the broader history described in earlier chapters: the idea that the actions of CPS are always situated within a wider context of harm that goes undiscussed.

In her account of the injustice of school closure, Ross referred back to the conditions under which many Bronzeville schools were constructed in the first place—the extreme segregation discussed in chapter 2, which drove CPS to open new buildings for black students rather than allow them to attend school elsewhere. For her those conditions meant that the buildings were always constructed on a faulty premise—the need to contain black students rather than the need to educate them. "They were just putting up these factory schools. With no input from the community. Why? Because the community was black. And poor. . . . If you look at it, the schools in the projects are the ones that closed first. 'Oh, project schools, projects are no longer here, oop! Do away with the school.' But if they would have thought about making these community schools in the first place, you wouldn't have as many issues." For her closing the schools represents an ironic end to a cruel cycle of racism and disregard for black life that began before she was born. In both instances—the historical precedent and the present moment—the people who make the policy decisions are isolated from the fallout that follows them. They do not have to live in the affected communities or, because of the massive bureaucratic structure built around these policy decisions, to accept personal responsibility or even acknowledge their a role in them. For those living within the Veil, the feeling is maddening. The reality you know to be true, because you witnessed it and everyone you know and love is still facing the consequences, goes unacknowledged.

Roberts, the local business leader, argued adamantly that the focus on academic test scores during the hearings was "insulting." He believed that if CPS had focused purely on a resource-based argument rather than comparing test scores that were not substantially different in any way, residents would have been more amenable to change.

> "Well, these kids are failing anyway." Don't do that! Don't do it! Just take it strictly from the business part of it and tell people, if we can close this school and take your kids to a school four blocks away, now those kids are gonna have a full library, nurse, arts program, everything. We can move it there. Keep that narrative. And then people would say, "Oh, I'm leaving my school even though my granddaddy went there, I went there, this is gonna be better because they're bringing over all the resources." And *do* something. Put new windows in. Do what you gotta do. Just make it nice. And then you ingratiate people. People aren't blind, really, that much. But they always have to add the insult. . . . Just leave it alone. It's always a comparison [between schools' test scores].

He also felt that when accused of racism, CPS should have offered an honest acknowledgment of history rather than trying to skirt the issue. Since it was an open secret that school closings were the culmination of a much longer sequence of historical events, failing to admit that—pretending instead that it was a matter of test scores or mysteriously empty buildings—came across as disrespectful and duplicitous. This, in turn, only furthered the idea that CPS could not be trusted.

> I think they should have just said, "*Yes*, this is a race issue, because the projects were built because of racial bias. So when the

projects came down, it affects black people more than [white] people in Lincoln Park." And it is a racial issue. Don't dodge it. And the schools that are being closed are in black areas for a reason. Look at the history. . . . To me, if you strike people with the truth, swift and hard, then they have a different perspective of you.

This last comment, about CPS's failure to "strike people with the truth," leads to another important theme that emerged from Bronzeville residents' mourning stories: the idea that honorable people should live by a moral code, and that CPS and the mayor were dishonorable and deceitful because they failed to do so. Reflecting Chicago's deeply entrenched history of street organizations and organized crime, some participants characterized Mayor Emanuel as a gang leader beholden to his "cronies" instead of to average citizens, deploying district employees as "enforcers."[25]

McNealy put it explicitly, framing average Chicagoans as innocents caught in the cross fire and terrorized by city leaders who act like gang kingpins. "They ain't worried about the consequences. They worried about how much more money I'ma get. This is a big hit. They talk about the gangsters, they talk about Al Capone, they talk about the Vice Lords, they talk about the [Gangster] Disciples. But this government is the worst example of interrogating and railroading the people, and gangsters. We [average people] don't have nobody." Describing the mayor, Prentice said, "He's just trying to collect his money, he's just trying to get his. And whoever is in on it, they get theirs. And they just go about their day and stay quiet." Roberts said of district employees, "They don't care. They get their $150,000 or $160,000 a year to enforce things." These uses of gang imagery are complicated, because for many Chicagoans gangs are an embedded part of social life, not a distinct criminal class but a set of multigenerational social bonds.[26] Thus the mayor's transgression was not his *being* a gang leader, but his failure to *act honorably* within the ethical logic of gang social codes—in contrast to his predecessor, Mayor Richard M. Daley, who was seen as a "real" gangster. "And no matter what people outside Chicago say," said Roberts, "people in Chicago respect that. Because this is a gangster town."

Richard Collins, the director of a community nonprofit in Bronzeville, made a similar unfavorable comparison between Rahm Emanuel and "real" gangster Richard M. Daley:

> What [Emanuel is] doing isn't drastically different—in some ways it is. I mean, he just doesn't care. Appearance means nothing. He's doing the same stuff: Daley closed schools, Rahm closed schools. Daley tore down public housing, Rahm's tearing down public housing. Daley was cookin' the books, Rahm's cookin' the books. It's the same thing. It's just, what Rahm is doing is so egregious that it's hard to look the other way. It's like, you know, everybody knows that the Mafia kills people. But you just can't kill people in broad daylight and not expect anything to happen. . . . It's like dude, I'm with you, but dag!

Much like Ross's characterization of school closings as "blatant," Collins here is suggesting that the mayor is not adhering to "the Chicago way," a political tradition that embraces a certain amount of cronyism, nepotism, and corruption but expects one to be discreet or at least maintain the appearance of propriety. In contrast to Daley's behind-the-scenes dealings, Emanuel's actions are seen as disrespectful, like committing murder in broad daylight. This distinction is partly a matter of scale; although his predecessor closed dozens of schools in the decade before Emanuel was elected, the move to close so many schools at once was unprecedented.[27]

In an era when national attention has been fixed on "Chicago violence" within a relatively narrow framework—observable gun violence—Bronzeville residents are attuned to a form of violence that is less direct and less immediately visible but no less lethal: structural violence.[28] This form of violence creates systems within which death and despair are quiet but inevitable, and the weapons at hand are history, policy, and racism. And regardless of what the outside world may think about the quality or worth of closed schools as "failing institutions," their role as crucial pillars of their communities means their wanton destruction is a key step in enacting such structural violence.

And to make matters worse, those most harmed by structural violence are those who feel least empowered to stop it. Warner said she felt that the district was implicitly telling her and other teachers, "'You're just stupid women. Shut up and do what we tell you to do.' That's the attitude that comes from downtown and comes from the mayor's office." And Moss said of the school closing hearings, "It was already decided pretty much. I mean, I don't think it mattered what we said. I really don't believe it mattered at all."[29]

Despite this feeling of voicelessness, the Bronzeville teachers I spoke with emphatically said they believed they were responsible for helping children make meaning of school closure, even as they themselves were mourning. Baker was concerned about students' repeating the language of failure they heard in the news media, rhetoric that positioned them (and their low test scores) as being to blame for the loss of their school. In her current teaching position, where many of her students had been displaced from their previous schools, she invited them to share their feelings about what happened. "Many of them remember the school closings and how they felt about it. . . . It's interesting what they say. They're like, 'Yeah, the schools were closed because we're black and we were failing all our tests.' And it's like, 'Well, actually you know, the schools were closed because they were underutilized.' And they're like, 'But we weren't—there were kids everywhere!' So how do you explain that to someone?"

In the days between the announcement of potential closure and the final decision, Moss says, she and other teachers tried to mask their own feelings to better support the young people around them. "You know, I think we tried to put a nice face on it. . . . 'You'll have new teachers, but I'm sure those teachers are going to care about you as well.' Do you know what I mean? I don't think we sat there and, like, tried to paint an even uglier picture. We didn't want to exacerbate their anxiety or their fear or their pain of loss. Because they were feeling loss too."

Three of the five teachers I spoke with expressed hesitation and fear about growing attached to another school and perhaps facing additional trauma. A fourth teacher did not discuss such reluctance openly but has left teaching for another field altogether. Among those who mentioned it explicitly, I was struck that they spoke of this reluctance using a language of intimacy and vulnerability, as if they'd experienced romantic or other interpersonal heartbreak. Katherine Warner, the teacher who said she would not "ever recover" from losing her school, described how difficult it was for her to fit in at the school she went to next. Even though it was near the closed school and served a similar student population, she had a hard time working with the students, faculty, and administration. "I was in tears with my principal at [the new school]. Because he was like, 'I don't know how to make this better with you.' And I said . . . , you know, I was so heartbroken after what they did to [the closed school] that to open myself up, to be that integral part of a school again? I don't know [if] I could do it."

Lynn Ross also compared her commitment and intense social bonding at the closed school with a much different sense of herself at her new school, an academically competitive school on the South Side. "At my old school I felt like, I'ma give you everything, and I'ma stay till seven o'clock at night. And you can sit in here if you don't wanna go home. . . . [But] after everything that happened with Emerson, I was like, "I have spent five years of my life doing this, and it's gone. So what am I going to . . . I need to figure out what's going to fulfill me, because clearly this can be gone. Any day, any time. . . . I loved doing what I do and it's gone." Ross's boundless warmth toward her students, her willingness to "give you everything," was curtailed when the experience of loss made her realize that the social bonds she thrived on might be temporary and could be taken away.

Amanda Moss, too, had a hard time handling the move to a new school (which would ultimately close as well). "That first year was really, really rough. I was unhappy, I didn't want to be there. This was not my choice, right? I was sort of mourning, I guess, my loss." When news came down that this school also faced closure, Moss felt, based on her previous experience, that trying to resist was pointless. "It was already decided, and they were just going through the motions. The downtown people, not the people on the ground, but the downtown people were just going through the motions, saying 'we're going to have a hearing and decide.' So that's when I started applying to graduate schools." Now Moss is a substitute teacher and uses the flexible schedule to establish a singing career rather than continuing as a classroom teacher after nine years in the district. "At this point I don't envision myself going back to teaching full time. I don't really trust . . . the students that I would want to teach, I just don't trust the system to allow me to teach them."

GHOSTS IN THE CITY

These are mourning stories,[30] which in a sense makes them ghost stories. The changes in Bronzeville have been made with the promise of a positive metamorphosis. But as urban planner Janet

Smith and education scholar David Stovall have written, these "discourses of 'transformation' and 'renaissance' evoke such promise for the new gentry, but a counter-story is omitted, or masked."[31] In a way, ghost stories serve as an important counterstory; a ghost story says *something you thought was gone is still happening here*; a ghost story says *those who are dead will not be forgotten*.[32] Something, someone, is still here. We are still here, despite all attempts to eradicate us. This defies the dominant narrative of the city's powerful, who would prefer to position the destruction of black institutions as a necessary step toward beautification or marketability. Or, as a group of four black teenage poets put it during the 2014 Louder Than a Bomb Teen Poetry Slam Festival,[33]

> Hammer in one hand, paintbrush in the other
> Rahm Emanuel singlehandedly destroying our city
> Mister Wreck-It Rahm
> Look at what Chicago's becoming
> Bending the rules to fit a lie of building a new Chicago
> Building new streets when your own plan got some potholes
> Tearing down dreams
> It's getting real windy in these streets
> Where Xs mark the spot where his wrecking ball is next to drop
> We are not included in the blueprint of the new Chicago
> We're being pushed out
> Our buildings being transformed into condos
> And we know those ain't for us.

And of course we aren't the only city with ghosts. In his account of the closure of his historic New York City alma mater (an essay with the online title "The Life and Death of Jamaica High School"), Jelani Cobb describes visiting the old building and finding it covered in tarps. "It looked," he writes, "as if it were draped in a shroud."[34] Sociologist Marcus Anthony Hunter describes the contemporary black Seventh Ward in Philadelphia as a "graveyard," a site of collective black memory where residents honor the institutions they have lost.[35] Journalist Gene Demby describes taking a friend on a walking tour around his native Philadelphia, only to find that the school he once attended is no more.

> Memory was the only place that Durham—my Durham—still existed. The school had closed its doors in the late 1990s because of the city's crushing budget problems, and was later swept up in a wave of charterization that took over Philly after I graduated. The old Durham building now housed something called the Independence Charter School. . . . It was a peculiar sense of loss that I felt the day I visited Durham—one of unmooring.[36]

Judith Butler argues that when a community faces the loss of a place, that loss can become so insurmountable that it becomes part of the community's own self-definition, "where community does not overcome the loss, where the community *cannot* overcome the loss without losing the very sense of itself as community."[37] Understanding these tropes of death and mourning as they pertain not to the people we love, but to the places where we loved them, has a particular gravity during a time when the deaths of black people at the hands of the state—through such mechanisms as police violence and mass incarceration—are receiving renewed attention. As the people of Bronzeville understand, the death of a school and the death of a person at the barrel of a gun are not the same thing, but they also *are* the same thing. The people of Bronzeville understand that a school is more than a school. A school is the site of a history and a pillar of black pride in a racist city. A school is a safe place to be. A school is a place where you find family. A school is a home. So when they come for your schools, they're coming for you. And after you're gone, they'd prefer you be forgotten.

Mourning, then, is how we refute that erasure. It's a way to insist that we matter. It's a way to remember.

Conclusion: An Open Door

> I gave him the letter to read and when he finished he said, "You go, my child; you're the one to go, for you have the story to tell." It seemed like an open door in a stone wall.
>
> —Ida B. Wells, *Crusade for Justice: The Autobiography of Ida B. Wells*

On a fall afternoon, I stop at my favorite bakery on 47th Street. The last time I was here, the boy working behind the counter was a newly graduated eighth grader pulling summer duty at the family business. Now he's a freshman at a school not far from here. His grandfather watches as he rings up my peach cobbler, standing by the faded calendars, handwritten signs, and newspaper clippings of glowing reviews from over the years. "I swear you grew three inches over the summer!" I exclaim. The boy blushes and nods slightly, handing me my change and assuring me that so far high school is going well. In Bronzeville, a visit to a place like this—a family-owned business, or an artist's workspace, or the park on a sunny day—can make you feel lost in time, as if the community has stood still while the rest of the world rushes forward. And yet though much remains the same, so much has changed. Where high-rise projects stood, vast stretches of grass or concrete sprawl toward the horizon. Where children once ran and tumbled and called to one another, playgrounds sit empty, overlooked by darkened windows. Mayo is gone. Williams is gone.

Overton is gone. The State Street Corridor is gone. With it, so many families have gone. What remain are questions and stories and the people who keep them.

What do school closures, and their disproportionate clustering in communities like Bronzeville, tell us about a fundamental devaluation of African American children, their families, and black life in general? Is there room for democracy and real grassroots participation in a school system that has been run like an oligarchy?

When Barbara Byrd-Bennett made her statement to the board, she encouraged them—and anyone else who might be listening, including journalists and average citizens—to see Chicago's empty school buildings as a "utilization crisis," a matter of dire urgency demanding immediate attention.

> Every year that we delay to take an action on our utilization crisis means another year of loss, another year of hope dimmed. That is why we need to move immediately to consolidate the schools, meeting the utilization committee's criteria, and to move students to schools that provide them with better opportunities to succeed.

Within this frame, the frame of the *utilization crisis*, school closure indeed appears to be the only option for anyone who cares about children. If these underutilized school buildings are dimming hopes, of course any educator or citizen with a conscience ought to want them closed. That is the picture Byrd-Bennett is painting. In this picture it makes no sense to defend these buildings or argue against shutting down these schools.

But if we consider not only the painting but the frame, we might come to other conclusions because we have seen that, when considering a school's value, there is more to the assessment than meets the eye. There is the symbolic weight of a school as a bastion of community pride, and also the fear that losing the school means conceding a battle in a much larger ideological war over the future of a city and who gets to claim it. There is the need to consider that losing the school represents another assault in a long line of racist attacks against a people, part of a history of levying harmful policies against them, blaming them for the aftermath, then having the audacity to pretend none of it really happened. There is the way some of these policy decisions are camouflaged by pseudoscientific analysis that is both ethically and statistically questionable. There is our intensely segregated society to account for, in which those who attend the school experience a fundamentally different reality than those who have the power to steer its future. And finally, there is the intense emotional aftermath that follows school closure, which can have a profound, lasting effect on those who experience the closure even as it is rarely acknowledged with any seriousness by those who made the decision.

It's worth stating explicitly: my purpose in this book is not to say that school closures should never happen. Rather, in expanding the frame within which we see school closure as a policy decision, we find ourselves with a new series of questions about Byrd-Bennett's claims, and about the district's decision more broadly. These questions, I contend, need to be asked about Chicago's school closures, about school closures anywhere. In fact, they are worth asking when considering virtually any educational policy decision: What is the history that has brought us to this moment? How can we learn more about that history from those who have lived it? What does this institution represent for the communities closest to it? Who gets to make the decisions here, and how do power, race, and identity inform the answer to that question? In the case of Chicago, a city built upon a constantly evolving blueprint of segregation, asking such critical questions invariably brings us, one way or another, to the question of racism. And yet political leaders and decision makers are loath to have an honest conversation about the racism we still live with and the ways it may affect our current reality. Given that unwillingness, the next necessary step—figuring out how to dismantle these racist structures—feels very far away.

Our sense of choice is always guided and constrained by frames.[1] When faced with a problem, we can conceive of solutions only within the realm of what we understand to be possible. Of course, frames can also construct a problem where there was none, and the history of American education is full of "solutions" that were depicted as absolutely necessary in response to problems that perhaps never really existed. Consider, for instance, the practice, common in American schools of past eras, of forcing left-handed children to write with their right hands. Or, more insidious, consider the practice of forcing American Indian children in boarding schools to speak English rather than their indigenous languages. Children's writing with their left hands or speaking indigenous languages is not inherently a problem; in these cases the frames *invented* problems by construing these actions as deviant or threatening.[2]

In other instances the problem at hand may be real, but the frame we are presented with limits our ideas for solving it. In the case of school closures, the wide array of issues that Byrd-Bennett presents as problems for Chicago's students—low graduation rates, a lack of arts instruction, limited access to nurses and counselors—are real and troubling. But by presenting them as somehow caused by building underutilization, the district limits the terms of engagement. Within this frame, instead of asking "How can we best address these problems?" the question becomes

"Are you going to address the utilization crisis or not?" The crisis itself is taken as fact, as is its role in causing these problems.

And while it would be easy to see the 2013 school closures as over and done with, their aftermath leaves several challenges at our feet. How can we address the lingering anguish and frustration created by the closure process? What should we do with the vacant school buildings across the city that have yet to be repurposed? How can we address the fact that enrollment in the district has indeed dropped precipitously in recent years? Should we close more schools? If so, how should we go about closing them in a way that minimizes trauma? Or do we leave all schools open in perpetuity? What lessons can we draw from the entire process that might be applied to other school policy questions in the future?

What do we do?

The answer to that question is complicated, in no small part because it depends on who "we" is, and because it requires making changes to a deeply entrenched institutional structure. Public education has emerged as one of the most contentious areas of public policy and debate in Chicago, with some of the most frustrating and harmful instances of policy malfeasance. At the same time, it is an arena where activists and organizers have also shown remarkable capacity for resistance, change, and transformation. With ongoing pressure, participation, collaboration, and a demand for accountability from those in power, perhaps CPS can learn from the school closures to create structures that let stakeholders participate meaningfully in decisions so as to incorporate community voices and proceed with care the next time a school closure—or any major policy decision—is on the table. CPS dates back to the mid-nineteenth century, when Chicago was a city of about thirty thousand. In the time since, the city's population has grown to ninety times that number. The neighborhood boundaries, racial composition, social fabric, political life, and economy of the city have all evolved, as they have elsewhere in America. As CPS looks ahead to another 150 years, continued change is inevitable. It's certainly unrealistic to expect that all schools as we know them will stay open forever. Assuming that school closure or consolidation and the construction of new schools are inevitable, how can CPS and other school districts undertake these changes in ethical ways?

However, when an institution has displayed a consistent history of racist and oppressive tactics, and when it is inextricably bound up in broader systems that are unjust, it may be impossible to transform it from within. In this case it becomes necessary to focus on resisting and dismantling the structures that make up the institution. CPS is currently structured to minimize opportunities for meaningful community-informed decision making. The superintendent and the members of the school board are unilaterally appointed by the mayor, without restriction. In its long-term history, CPS has a demonstrated record of maintaining segregation and inequality. In its more recent history, the mayor's leadership shows a general disregard for equity or for the transformative change that might get us there. In a city like Chicago, notorious for its corruption and widely undemocratic in most of its functioning, this is unlikely to change.

There is plenty of evidence that CPS is an institution too steeped in its own racist history to ever truly transform. Even within its very recent history, the school district was designed to actively maintain segregated schools. Aside from the fact of segregation itself, this mode of functioning indicates something more nefarious: the belief that black children do not deserve a high-quality education. Furthermore, there are myriad ways CPS enacts harmful policies that I have not discussed in depth because they go beyond the purview of this book, but that create the backdrop for it. They include the fact that suspension and expulsion are still disproportionately high among black students; the budget changes that have left students with disabilities to fend for themselves without the support they are legally entitled to;[3] the fact that two-thirds of the police officers assigned to patrol CPS schools have previous conduct complaints on file.[4]

And, of course, this logic was not invented by CPS. Across the country, at the highest levels of decision-making power, we see education policies that value neoliberal ideologies over the lives of children—especially when the children are black. Even if CPS were able to undergo a radical transformation, it would still be situated within a system that prioritizes market logic and privatization and has demonstrated a lack of commitment to ensuring that all children have what they need to be successful in school.

And so, once more, what do we do?

A few days after the 2016 presidential election, when many across America were feeling confused, dejected, and hopeless, I attended an event that featured a conversation with education scholar and activist Bill Ayers. Ayers spoke of the freedom fighters who were active in South Africa during the days of apartheid, struggling every day with their minds, their hearts, and their lives to end a system that had been in place for as long as anyone could remember, governing every aspect of day-to-day life. It must have seemed impossible to topple the system even as people understood intuitively that they could not go on like that forever. Nevertheless, they took time to envision life after apartheid, to dream of what would come next. "We do a good job of critiquing the world as it is," said Ayers, "but we don't always do a good job of positing what we're fighting for."

When it comes to public schools in Chicago, the injustices are so numerous and have such a persistent hold on our lives that we could spend all our energy thinking about how to tear them down and our ideas would still feel inadequate. Every day, I find myself mindful of a new wrong being committed against the children of the city I call home, and some days it feels as if those wrongs will continue to cascade ceaselessly until they've drowned me and everyone I love.

On those days I think of *Romeo and Juliet*. When I was a middle school language arts teacher, I received a grant to teach a unit on *Romeo and Juliet* for my eighth-grade homeroom class. I brought together every tool I could think of to make the experience educational, personally enriching, affirming, challenging, and engaging for the class. They were in charge of casting and directing the play, interpreting and rehearsing the script, designing and constructing props, costumes, and sets, and hosting talkbacks with younger students after the play. It became one of those experiences that keeps every teacher going—the chance to witness the moment of revelation, of "it was hard but I did it," of love enacted.

Other days, I think of my visit to a public school on the Yurok Indian Reservation in northern California, a trip I made as part of a research project requested by the National Indian Education Association and supported by the Harvard University Native American Program. The school I visited had been designed with community input so that students were being assessed not only by statewide standards, but also on things that mattered to people in the community, such as Yurok language instruction and relationships with elders. In one classroom I visited, students studying math curled up in comfortable nooks around the room. Some worked in small groups, some with the teacher, some on their own, and some with a "class grandmother"—an elder in the community, integrated as a valued actor in the educational experience rather than kept out based on some strict school/community binary. The students I spoke to were grounded in a sense of self and a sense of heritage; they were proud, and they were learning.

I return to moments like this because they remind me of what is possible in schools. In addition to taking honest account of the many ways school districts get things wrong, we must continually set our sights on what it would look like to get things right, and we must integrate those visions into our rhetoric and our strategy. "It is our dreams that point the way to freedom," wrote the poet Audre Lorde.[5]

Dreams can be hard to sustain, especially when the world around you seems hell-bent on destroying them. When asked how community members he works with have experienced school closures, Richard Collins, the nonprofit leader I spoke with in chapter 4, explained how Bronzeville residents' emotional responses to pain and loss caused some to shut down emotionally:

> As resilient people, as I would imagine is the case for most oppressed people around the world, you're constantly used to adapting to the new normal. Nothing is ever stable. *Nothing* is ever stable . . . And so instability is the norm. . . . It's stressful. It's emotionally tumultuous to experience the loss of your housing, or your school for your child, or the loss of your child, or your child experiencing the loss of one of their friends to violence. But we have to do it every day. And so there's an aspect of us that does become dehumanized. Because we can't. It's like, who in their right mind would deal with that kind of a letdown? You'd go crazy. And so we cut off parts of ourselves.[6]

In a sense, for Bronzeville and communities like it across the city and across America, this is what the fight against school closures is really about. It's about understanding oneself as a character in a seemingly interminable tragedy, one who staggers across the stage over and over again, act after act—and deciding to try to interrupt the supposed death sentence you've been handed. It's a fight to say *not one more, not here, not today.* It's a fight to say *you did this to my grandaddy and now you're trying to do it to me, and I say not again*. This, we insist, is our home. Broken though it may be, it remains beautiful, and we remain children of this place. We insist on a right to claim it, to shape it, to keep it. We took the freedom train to get here. Might as well do the work to get free.

ACKNOWLEDGMENTS

This book would not have been possible without the emotional support, wise counsel, careful attention, and tireless encouragement of innumerable individuals, whom I will nevertheless try my best to enumerate. I've relied on the vision, guidance, candor, and straight-up hustle of my editor, Elizabeth Branch Dyson, a hero in my eyes for her commitment to the book, for her deep understanding of why this work matters, and for her willingness to do important things an editor ought to do, like tell me when I'm being boring. Thank you as well to Dylan Montanari, Levi Stahl, Alice Bennett, and everyone at the University of Chicago Press.

I am incredibly grateful for the support of all my colleagues at the University of Chicago School of Social Service Administration. Thank you especially to Deborah Gorman-Smith, who created an environment where I felt supported in this seemingly monumental task and provided the resources for me to host a manuscript workshop to support the book's development, and to Charles Payne, a titan in the world of education who, when I first told him about this book, got a twinkle in his eye that made me believe it could be written. During my manuscript workshop, I received feedback that was at once demanding, exacting, and generous from Amanda Lewis, Omar McRoberts, Mary Pattillo, and William Sites.

They brought their own particular perspectives and an uncompromising belief in my ability to make this book as good as it could possibly be, and I am grateful for that. Logistical support and notes were provided during the workshop by the wonderful Bridgette Davis, Ebony Hinton, and Marion Malcome.

Thank you to my graduate committee, who saw this work in its early iterations and shepherded it along the way. Thank you to Sara Lawrence-Lightfoot, my North Star, who continually awes me as a model of masterful storytelling, attentive questioning, independent creativity, good humor, and joy. She gives me courage to write the way I write. From her I've drawn lessons I think will take years to understand, and I'm ready to put in the time. Roberto Gonzales has been a source of constant cheer, a generous problem solver, and a mentor with a "let's go for it!" spirit that has gotten me through much uncertainty. William Julius Wilson has always challenged me to read more, write more, think harder, and be clearer, and to do so with boldness. In their own ways, these three have all left their mark on this manuscript, and on me—not only in the scholarly lineage of the sources I cite or the theories I draw from, but in their way of being, which in all three is fierce, brilliant, and sometimes irreverent. For that, and for them, I am grateful.

I have been blessed with a family that has always believed in me and supported me any way they could. Thank you to my parents, Sylvia Ewing and Dean Ewing, for loving me unconditionally and constantly fretting that I work too hard (they're wrong). Thank you to my mother in particular for reading my book proposal and a sample chapter before I sent them to the press. Always, I am striving to write a book that my mother will find to be good, and that will live up to the dreams she carries for our city. Thank you to my husband, Damon Jones, who spent some of our first dates listening patiently to my incoherent ravings about "efficiency formulas." I am blessed to have a partner who, without fail, supports me, urges me forward when I feel like giving up, believes in me, gives wonderful and thoughtful advice, understands what it takes to make a book a book, and has my back no matter what.

Thank you to Sylvester, to Matthew, to John and Zara, to Mumsi, to Grandad (who I think has read more of my writing over the years than any living person other than myself, and done so with undue care), to Grandma and Grandpa, to Jean-Luc, to all my aunts and uncles, to Arlin, to Dylan, to all my cousins, and most especially to Leila, who inspires so very much of what I do.

Thank you to my many brilliant, kind, attentive friends and partners in scholarship, and to the colleagues who gave me feedback and listened to nascent ideas, encouraged me, mentored me, and provide models of how to unite love, justice, and rigor: Abena Mackall, Adrienne Keene, Adom Getachew, Alan Mather, Barbara Ransby, Bill Ayers, Carla Shedd, Cathy Cohen, Celia Gomez, Clint Smith, Danielle Roper, Daniel Kay Hertz, David Stovall, Deepa Vasudevan, Hubert Morgan, Jasson Perez, Jessica Baker, John B. Diamond, Jonathan Rosa, Laurence Ralph, Lizzie Adelman, Marc Lamont Hill, Matthew Shaw, Michael Dumas, R. L'Heureux Lewis-McCoy, Shauna Leung, Stephany Cuevas, Tracye Matthews, Yanilda María González, and Zandria Robinson. Thanks especially to Elizabeth Todd-Breland both for her friendship and for her generous assistance in the wonderful world of CPS archives.

Thank you to the writers in my life who are also my dear friends, who console me without fail and take turns telling me to push forward or to give myself a break: Amanda Torres, Fatimah Asghar, Hanif Abdurraqib, José Olivarez, Josie Duffy, Kiese Laymon, Kristiana Colón, Natalie Moore, Nate Marshall, Vann Newkirk, and Ydalmi Noriega.

Thank you to all the people of Bronzeville, especially Anna Jones, Erana Jackson Taylor, Irene Robinson, Jawanza Malone, all of the Dyett hunger strikers, and all those in Chicago and beyond who supported them. Thank you to all of my colleagues at Pershing West Middle School, most especially my principal, Cheryl Watkins, who saw something in me and thought, "This person could be a good teacher." Thank you to all of my Pershing students, who are still my babies even as they grow up tall and even have babies of their own.

Early versions of this manuscript received valuable feedback from the members of the Association of Black Sociologists and of the Race, Ethnicity, Migration, and Inequality Working Group at the Harvard Graduate School of Education. Thank you to Sarah Hainds, Carol Caref, and everyone at the Chicago Teachers Union, especially the research team. Thank you to Bradford Hunt, who provided generous assistance with chapter 2. Thank you to Anne Heminger and Damon Jones for helping me obtain elusive population data. Thank you to Jaida Nabayan, Layla West, and Nadirah Farah Foley for helping put the finishing touches on the manuscript. Thank you to the one and only Tabia Yapp for making it possible for so many of my ideas to float around in the world.

Thank you to the social sciences reference staff at the Harold Washington Library, the staff of the Vivian G. Harsh Archives at the Carter G. Woodson Public Library, and all the staff at the University of Chicago Library and the Boston Public Library.

Thank you to the top-notch journalists of the city of Chicago, especially those few who maintain a keen focus on educational issues, such as Kalyn Belsha, Sarah Karp, Linda Lutton, and Becky Vevea. Linda in particular has been a hero to me and I literally could not have written this book without her work. Thank you also to my colleagues at the University of Chicago Consortium on School Research, whose robust scholarship laid the foundation for much of what is contained here.

Thank you to the countless individuals, most of whom I will never meet, who make up my social media community. Thanks for your cheers, your good questions, your generous support, and your completely unreasonable and astonishing care. I am grateful for this odd and incredible thing we do, trying to be there for people we don't even really know.

Thank you to the ancestors, named and forgotten, whose brilliance and strength, courage and creativity, set the blueprint for all my best efforts. Thank you to everyone who got on the train and rode north. Thank you for making for us a home here.

APPENDIX

Methodological and Theoretical Notes

This book is derived from research I conducted between 2014 and 2016, though informally it all began in 2013 the moment I read the newspaper article I describe in the introduction and learned that the school where I had taught was going to be closed. The study is a textbook example of the dynamic and evolving nature of research endeavors. I set out thinking I simply wanted to interview people affected by school closures and understand how they conceptualized race, racism, and their role in education policy decisions. (It was during these interviews that the concept of institutional mourning unexpectedly emerged.) On the advice of a mentor, I made the decision early on to focus on one community and go deep, rather than try to write about the entire city or even the entire South Side. As I pushed myself to better understand the context of what had happened in 2013, I chose to pursue the four paths that became the four chapters of this book.

The account in chapter 1 is drawn from my notes at eighteen hours of public events pertaining to Dyett, such as rallies, press conferences, and vigils, and at public events where Dyett was discussed, such as a hearing held by CPS and a Chicago Board of Education meeting. The biographical details on the life of Walter H. Dyett come from his personal archival papers.

The historical analysis in chapter 2 is derived from my review of data from CPS records and CHA records, as well as excellent secondary sources on the histories of these two institutions and of the city overall, especially black Chicago. In particular, H. Bradford Hunt's *Blueprint for Disaster: The Unraveling of Chicago Public Housing* was an immensely helpful text.

The discourse analysis in chapter 3 makes use of audio files recorded by WBEZ, the local public radio affiliate, of all the school closure hearings, which journalist Linda Lutton almost single-handedly attended and taped, posting the recordings on the website of our local public radio affiliate. I'm so glad she did. The transcriptions of these audio files were variably done by me or by an outside transcriptionist and were subsequently coded by me using NVIVO.

The theoretical ideas presented in chapter 4 are based on interviews with thirteen individuals affiliated with closed schools as teachers, parents, students, or community members, selected for their ability to share a variety of representative perspectives. They represent six closed schools, and three of them (two teachers and one student) experienced multiple consecutive school closures. These interviews took place between July 2015 and January 2016, and each lasted one to two hours. I used a semistructured interview protocol, included later in this appendix.

VOICE AS WITNESS

In this book I strive to tell *a* story, rather than *the* story. I tell this story as someone neither at the center of its events nor invisible to its participants, from my vantage point as someone literally and figuratively observing not from outside the action, but from its borders. As Lawrence-Lightfoot and Davis describe, a researcher who endeavors to create a portrait uses her voice in many ways. One way the researcher's voice can enter the work is *voice as witness*. In this manner the researcher takes a stance as "as discerning observer. . . . We see the portraitist standing on the edge of the scene—a boundary sitter."[1]

What does it mean to be a boundary sitter? One of my favorite paintings is *Nightlife*, by Archibald Motley[2]—a black artist who is often discussed as a Harlem Renaissance painter although he lived and worked in Chicago. The painting depicts a Bronzeville nightclub packed with revelers: black people in stylish clothes dancing, throwing their heads back in laughter, leaning in for close conversation, pondering their troubles over a drink. I like the way Motley leaves us just at the edge of the action. We're close enough that it seems we can hear the jazz and the chattering voices, smell the cigarette smoke and wafting perfume, but we're also set back enough to observe the whole scene. We're not the bartender serving a foaming glass of beer, nor are we the clueless passersby fully outside the world of the painting. We sit in between, taking it all in and marveling at details that might otherwise be hard to catch—the small things like the way ash gathers at the tip of a man's cigar, and the bigger things like the red-purple light bathing everyone's skin. This, to me, is what it means to be a boundary sitter, to exercise voice as witness.

This position may be familiar to any social scientist whose work is contingent on the art of keen observation, but it has additional layers of meaning within the tradition of African American storytelling, where witnessing and testifying are important collective rituals. "In the oral tradition of Black English," writes literary scholar Yvonne Atkinson, "Witness and Testify go hand in hand: one who Witnesses has an obligation to Testify. . . . Witness/Testify is a shared collective memory, a cultural ritual that promotes solidarity and cohesion, creating a living archive of African American culture."[3] In African American religious tradition from slavery to the present, witnessing and testifying serve an important countercultural purpose: as oppression and white supremacy seemingly reign, she who testifies declares that she has nevertheless seen the blessings of the divine in her own life and still believes in the promise of freedom.[4]

NOTES ON MY OWN SUBJECT POSITION

While it is common to discuss positionality from a relational or social perspective, one aspect of social position that often goes undiscussed—perhaps because it is awkward or uncomfortable—is the body. During this research I became very aware of how my physical presence as a small-framed black woman informed people's perceptions of me. At times it made it easy for me to go relatively unnoticed, which could be either beneficial (allowing me to quietly observe) or detrimental (making it hard to get someone's attention for a conversation). Other aspects of my position created a complexly interwoven insider-outsider status: I was a CPS teacher, but I'm not currently employed by the district. I'm black, but I'm light-skinned and some people perceive me as racially ambiguous. I'm from Chicago and save for my time in graduate school have lived on the South Side for all of my adult life, but I'm not *from* the South Side, and I have a strange hybrid accent that marks me as being from elsewhere (not the "up south" accent common in Bronzeville). I'm affiliated with the University of Chicago, which has a terrible reputation in the community for its role in redlining and "urban renewal," and at the time I began this study I was a graduate student at Harvard University. I'm also an outspoken lifelong Chicagoan with a rich array of personal relationships across communities, including family relationships. (More than once, partway through talking to participants I realized they knew someone in my family.) Throughout the world, but especially in Chicago, such relationships are paramount. As the famous local aphorism goes, "we don't want nobody nobody sent"—in other words, you're only as good as the people who will vouch for you. For all these reasons, I've come to believe that the way we often discuss the "insider/outsider" dichotomy fails to capture this complexity, and that perhaps other theoretical constructs (notably, intersectionality) are better suited for the task. Working through this research endeavor required me to be comfortable examining my own subject position as dynamic and complicated, and being honest with myself about the ways my relative power or lack thereof might affect my entry into a situation as an interviewer or an observer.

RECIPROCITY AND SOCIAL LIFE

I'm not sure it's ever possible for researchers to achieve full reciprocity—to give research participants objects or experiences equivalent to what they've received. However, in all of my interactions with participants I strove to maintain reciprocal relationships, which often meant that we interacted as friends or associates and that I took part in social life in a more or less "normal" way. All interviews were done over food, usually at a place the participant chose, and I did end up making some sacrifices in fitness and finances. We shared coffee, donuts, fried chicken, fruit, cold water, peach cobbler, and other wonderful foods that affirmed my choosing Chicago over Boston as a research site. Because I have a car, I often gave participants rides after the interviews. Having been dependent on Chicago's public transportation for most of my life, I was keenly aware of the difference a car makes, and I gladly drove participants home and to work. In one instance I took a participant to pick up her mother and her two brothers, then drove them all to Cook County Jail to visit her brother (a difficult trip by bus). I also did my best to provide emotional support and to help younger participants with things like job searches.

People in Chicago are friendly, people in Bronzeville are even friendlier, and sometimes observant strangers would chime in with opinions or advice. After an interview where a young man said he needed a job to support his mother, a man at the next table introduced himself and launched into a long speech about the importance of self-reliance. After an interview with a teacher at a restaurant, a woman at the next table—another teacher—jumped in to share her own extensive opinions on school closing and corruption in the city. I believe these individuals' willingness to join the conversation also reflected their perception of me as approachable rather than especially academic or authoritarian.

CRITICAL DISCOURSE ANALYSIS

I chose the events I analyze in chapter 3 because they provide a unique formal opportunity to observe how community members and district officials interact within a designated space using prepared responses. Because community meetings, hearings, and press conferences offer a chance to make public declarations in support of closing a school or keeping it open, they allow a view into the evidence these parties marshal to support their claims—and therefore a view into the underlying logic they find convincing and important to consider.

During these hearings, we see several examples of what Dana-Ain Davis labels *muted racism*. This occurs when people make statements that are subtly racist not because of what is said, but because of what is *not* said. As Davis describes it, muted racism can take three forms:[5]

- *Deflection*: arguing that some social dysfunction other than racism is at the root of a problem ("Sure, some people struggle to get a job, but the real issue is class, not race.")

- *Indexicality*: using coded words to make claims about racial categories without explicitly mentioning race ("We'd like to keep this neighborhood the way it is, with a certain type of families living here.")
- *Omission*: analyzing data that shows racial disparities without discussing racism as a plausible reason for those disparities ("Our black male students are getting suspended every week. We need to address their behavior issues.")

In each of the school closure hearings and meetings, participants are discussing, in broad strokes, the same factual series of events. However, their interpretive repertoires[6] are notably different. Interpretive repertoires include the "terminology, stylistic and grammatical features, preferred metaphors and figures of speech" that together help the speaker construct a certain version of events or representation of reality in order to ultimately pursue social objectives.

I analyzed comments from a Chicago Board of Education meeting that took place on April 3, 2013, during which CPS CEO Barbara Byrd-Bennett delivered prepared remarks to members of the board and assembled members of the public. I used a video recording of this statement (twenty-two minutes long) to conduct this analysis. I also analyzed audio recordings of six other events, community meetings, and public hearings held for Bronzeville elementary schools slated for closure in 2013: Overton, Williams, and Mayo.

An additional Bronzeville school, Pershing West Middle School, serving grades four to eight, was also closed during this period. Before my time in graduate school, I was a teacher at Pershing West Middle School; it was the principal, teachers, and students of Pershing West who spurred my interest in education policy and social inequality and who supported me with love and enthusiasm when I was admitted to Harvard. Although there's much I could say reflexively about the closing of Pershing West, I opted to omit it from this particular data analysis because of this exceptional relationship.

As I noted above, each of the of the audio recordings analyzed in chapter 3 was made by journalists from WBEZ and posted (along with all such events for schools slated for closure citywide) on a publicly available website for streaming or download. I also obtained digital copies of the materials distributed to attendees at these events (the notice sent to parents about the process, maps of proposed attendance boundaries, and so forth) and the official hearing officer's determination for each school, issued to the CEO after the public comment period and hearings were over.

The purpose of critical discourse analysis is not to psychoanalyze a speaker. The question is not, "What does this person *really* mean by saying this?" Of course I have no way of reading people's minds to answer that question. Rather, critical discourse analysis sees speech as a form of action. The question therefore becomes, "What is this person *doing* by saying this?" What claims are made or undone, what ideologies are revealed, what happens to the balance of power in this interaction?

Linguist Norman Fairclough, one of the most influential scholars of critical discourse analysis, has called on the field to use it as a tool not only to describe structures of injustice, but to develop strategies for addressing them. As Fairclough describes it, "Strategies have a strongly discursive character: they include imaginaries for change and for new practices and systems, and they include discourses, narratives, and arguments which interpret, explain, and justify the area of social life they are focused upon—its past, its present, and its possible future."[7] As we have seen in this chapter, community members' discourse about Mayo, Williams, and Overton introduces an alternative means of evaluating the very nature of what constitutes a quality school—one that emerges from the grass roots, not from the top down. The framework for evaluation they present through their discourse centers black children and black communities as constituents with voices that matter, and it acknowledges the racialized social system we live in. Perhaps that very discourse offers a first step toward schools that are truly just and oriented to those they serve.

NOTES ON INSTITUTIONAL MOURNING

I mention my own grieving briefly in chapter 4. In a sense this entire project represents my own mourning. It created a way for me to gather with others and talk about something that was causing me great pain. It allowed me to process, through analysis, a series of hurtful events that, at the outset, I did not understand at all. Like someone who stays up late researching a loved one's diagnosis or a bereaved person going through an older relative's papers and photos, I set out on the research as a way of understanding and managing my own emotional response. Every time I went home I spent less and less time in my old neighborhood of Logan Square, which has gentrified so that I can't recognize many parts of it and it feels inhospitable. As the process wore on and so much else was happening in Chicago—especially the violent reality of the deaths of Laquan McDonald, Ronnieman Johnson, Rekia Boyd, Quintonio LeGrier, Bettie Jones, and Sandra Bland—I began to mourn for my city as well.

The idea that individuals might mourn institutions or other intangible entities, much as we mourn people, is not new. In his classic essay "Mourning and Melancholia," Freud includes this in his definition of mourning: "Mourning is regularly the reaction to the loss of a loved person, *or to the loss of some abstraction which has taken the place of one [loved person]*, such as one's country, liberty, an ideal, and so on" (my emphasis).[8] Although it's tempting to talk about protest in terms of logic and strategy, emotions play a tremendous role in all social movements.[9] And in dealing with school closures, the metaphor of death frequently crops up. In her study of the closure of one school in Austin, Texas, anthropologist Amanda Walker Johnson describes the community's experience surrounding the closure as "a form of social and civic death," one "characterized by the loss of natality and history."[10] The idea of *social death*, a death that is spiritual or political rather than physical, has been extensively explored in the field of black studies. A lineage of theorists identified as "Afro-pessimists" frame all American social life as dimmed by the shadow of slavery—a shadow that makes real participatory citizenship functionally nonexistent for black people in America. Jared Sexton calls social death "another name for slavery and an attempt to think about what it comprises,"[11] a definition that both expands the concept of death beyond the loss of a physical human body and establishes a direct link between social death and the broader condition of black oppression in the United States.

None of the questions in the semistructured interview protocol I created mentioned death, dying, or mourning. Rather, I observed that death and mourning emerged repeatedly in participants' accounts. This did not itself surprise me. Mentions of death are common in public discourse around school closings, exemplified by Chicago Teachers Union president Karen Lewis's referring to Rahm Emanuel as the "murder mayor" because he was "killing schools"[12] and by the more recent headline, "Will school choice kill Chicago's neighborhood high schools?"[13] Johnson, in her study on the closure of a Texas high school, notes the expansive use of death as a metaphor in local reporting, through phrases such as "pass or perish," "slow dying," "struggling to survive," and "funeral."[14]

Nevertheless, I found it remarkable how often participants made broader references to feelings of loss and processes that were reminiscent of grieving, and it is from this repeated observation that the present theory emerges. In retrospect, perhaps I should have anticipated that mourning would be a theme in participants' accounts, given my own reflections on the grief and sorrow I experienced, as I wrote in a 2015 essay: "When I found out that the school where I taught would be closing, I was visiting my father in Florida for spring break, and I locked myself in the bedroom and cried like a little kid. I started replaying life there in my head, over and over, like a sappy montage in a bad movie."[15] But as Sara Lawrence-Lightfoot and Jessica Davis note in *The Art and Science of Portraiture*, "through documentation, interpretation, analysis, and narrative we raise the mirror."[16] In this case I had to raise the mirror to my participants first, in order to see a reflection of both my own experience and a broader phenomenon.

From an empirical perspective, the data I use in chapter 4 has some fairly obvious limitations: I spoke to a relatively small number of people; I was asking them to process their recollections rather than interviewing them about events as they were happening; I made contact with them through snowball sampling, so some of the participants I interviewed have social ties to one another. Their perspectives, as I present them, are in no way intended to be exhaustive or necessarily representative of average attitudes in the population. Rather, I intended to draw on their responses to construct a theoretical framework that I believe has broader applicability, in the hope that it illuminates something fundamental about the social process they experience and that it will prove useful to scholars working in other settings in the future, who can expand, test, and critique the ideas presented here.

William Julius Wilson and Anmol Chaddha suggest that while many qualitative researchers, particularly ethnographers, have a dichotomous view of whether there should be an inductive or a deductive relation between their empirical work and their theoretical preoccupations—that is, whether a good sociologist ought to enter the field armed with a clear theoretical lens that shapes observations or should develop a theoretical framework purely in response to the findings in the field—there can in fact be a nuanced—dialogic—relation between theory and empiricism rather than a dichotomous one. "[Some] studies start out with a deductive theory and end up generating theoretical arguments in an inductive process that integrates old theoretically derived ideas with new and unanticipated theoretical arguments based on data uncovered in the field research." Ultimately, the authors argue, "The extent to which work can withstand critical and prolonged scrutiny in the context of validation will be based in large measure on the researcher's creative insights in the discovery and integration of empirical findings and theoretical ideas."[17] Although the theoretical ideas I present were developed from insights in the field, they are bolstered by a body of existing literature on mourning and its functioning, and I hope that other scholars will determine whether, how, and to what extent they have veracity in other contexts.

SEMISTRUCTURED INTERVIEW PROTOCOL

Chapter 4 is based on a series of semistructured interviews. Although I adapted and added questions over the course of each interview, I began every session with the same protocol.

Personal background:

Where did you grow up?

Where does your family come from? How long have they been in Chicago?

Views on Bronzeville:

Describe the street where you grew up (or the street where you live now).

Has the neighborhood changed since you have lived here? If so, how?

If you had to choose three words to characterize Bronzeville, what would they be? Why?

Tell me about some of your experiences as a resident of (public housing complex, if applicable).

Who would you say has power in the community?

If you could be in charge of what Bronzeville would look like in ten years, what would you want the community to be like? What are your dreams for the community?

Would you raise a family here? (If applicable.)

How do people respond when you tell them you are from this area?

Views on schools and school closings:

Tell me about some of your experiences at (local Bronzeville school).

If you were the mayor, do you think you would have made the decision to close the schools? Why or why not?

How do you think the decision to close the schools was made?

How do you think CPS decided which schools to keep open and which to stay closed?

What would you like the (closed school) building to become?

Views on race and racism:

Some people, like Karen Lewis, argue that the school closings were racist. Others, like Barbara Byrd-Bennett, say they were not. What do you think?

How would you define racism? How can you tell if something is racist or not?

Do you have discussions about racism with friends, family, or coworkers?

ETIC CODES

In conducting the critical discourse analysis described in chapter 3, I began with a short list of etic codes drawn from the literature and my initial thoughts on what themes would emerge as significant. These codes were:

- black people/blackness
- deflection
- demographic change
- economic forces
- history
- indexicality
- metaphor
- omission
- politics/political power/political leaders
- positioning
- racism
- segregation

NOTES

INTRODUCTION

1. Reprinted by consent of Brooks Permissions. To hear Brooks read the poem and offer interpretive notes on its meaning and origin, see the American Academy of Poets, https://www.poets.org/poetsorg/text/archive-gwendolyn-brooks-reading-guggenheim-museum-1983.

2. Kelleher, "Chicago Schools."

3. Sfondeles and Spielman, "Rauner Delivers."

4. Massey and Denton, *American Apartheid*, 72.

5. This work is intended to be "place sensitive" sociology that "understands place not just as a backdrop to our social lives but also as an agentic player in our social lives" (Shedd, *Unequal City*, 8).

6. Wilson, *Truly Disadvantaged*, 3.

7. Yosso, "Whose Culture Has Capital?," 7.

8. For an excellent analysis of how various factors (e.g., building use, race, and neighborhood composition) were predictive of school closures in Chicago from 2000 to 2013, including comparison between the stated rationales for school closures of the Daley and Emanuel administrations, see Great Cities Institute, "Why These Schools?"

9. These schools were matched for attributes including capacity utilization, test scores, truancy, proportion of low-income students, mobility, and other key characteristics.

10. Additionally, nearly 40 percent of displaced students were enrolled in schools on academic probation. These findings were mirrored in a national study conducted by the Center for Research on Education Outcomes, which found that just under half of students attend an academically superior school after their school closes. Center for Research on Education Outcomes, *Lights Off*.

11. De la Torre et al., *School Closings in Chicago*, 2.

12. Lipman, Vaughan, and Gutierrez, "Root Shock," 3.

13. Bobo, Kluegel, and Smith, "Laissez-Faire Racism."

14. Bonilla-Silva, "What Is Racism," 21.

15. Ibid.

16. This is one way the focus on Chicago makes a particular kind of sense as a laboratory for thinking about how racism functions in the nation more

broadly. The social, economic, and political structure of the United States rests on a foundation of chattel slavery and indigenous genocide, so in the sense that the city is profoundly racist, it is true that Chicago is, as Robert Sampson calls it in the title of his 2012 book, the great American city.

17. Throughout this book, the names of individuals have been changed except where they are public officials or where they requested otherwise.

CHAPTER ONE

1. Fournier, "'Give Our District A Chance.'"
2. Burris, "Caddo Proposes Building Three, Closing Six Schools."
3. Inns, "Some AISD Schools May Shut Down."
4. Simon and Kelleher, "Should This School Be Saved?"
5. Du Bois, *Souls of Black Folk*, vii.
6. Pattillo, *Black on the Block*, 171.
7. "Portfolio" mirrors "CEO" as an example of the language of business, corporations, and markets creeping into public education.
8. Pattillo, "Everyday Politics," 41. See also Dixson, "Whose Choice?"
9. Lipman and Haines, "From Accountability to Privatization."
10. Karp, "Neighborhood High Schools."
11. While Brizard cited academic failure—not low enrollment—in his letter to parents as the reason Dyett would close, Phillips (which remains open at this time and is managed contractually by the nonprofit Academy for Urban School Leadership with some autonomy from the rest of the district) did not differ significantly in academic performance—both schools were considered "Level 3" schools (the lowest performance ranking, characterized as needing "intensive intervention"); in 2010 the graduation rate was 42.9 percent at Phillips and 37.2 percent at Dyett, and both schools had average ACT scores of about 14 from 2007 to 2010.
12. "Brizard."
13. Berliner, "Near Impossibility," 205. See also Granger, "No Child Left Behind."
14. Simon and Kelleher, "Should This School Be Saved?"
15. Griffin, "Aquila Griffin et al. to Arne Duncan and Russlynn Ali."
16. Fortino, "UIC Education Experts."
17. Stone, "Chicago City Hall Sit-in."
18. Griffin, "Aquila Griffin et al. to Arne Duncan and Russlynn Ali."
19. Alderman Will Burns played a strange role in this story. Initially he publicly supported keeping Dyett open, then he had a disagreement with the members of the Coalition. Although he had been widely viewed as politically up-and-coming with the mayor's favor on his side, he later left political office very suddenly to work for Airbnb, despite being a career politician with no business background to speak of.

20. Karp, "CPS Reverses Course."

21. Coalition to Revitalize Walter H. Dyett High School, "Walter H. Dyett."

22. The first group to speak was the Washington Park Athletic Community Academy (WPACA), the second was the Coalition to Revitalize Walter H. Dyett High School, and the third was Little Black Pearl.

WPACA made the first presentation, led by Charles Campbell, who served as principal for Dyett's last year. The Washington Park Athletic Community Academy would be "designed to prepare students for careers in sports and beyond, using sports themes and concepts." Campbell emphasized that although the school would focus on athletics, it would also prepare students for "the industries surrounding athletics," such as entrepreneurship and general management. He played several videos from sports and athletic professionals (all men of color) describing the "creative mind-set" and skills they used to succeed in their fields. "According to *Money* magazine and the US Department of Labor, all of these professions are expected to see major growth over the next decade," Campbell said. The WPACA proposal expounds on these career development aspirations:

"Our vision is to motivate, engage and cultivate students through athletics while producing capable, confident graduates who are empowered to create the trajectory of their own future. The vision strategy is to make learning real for all students through engaging and innovative practices based in sports methodologies and concepts. The culture of WPACA develops students into exceptionally qualified candidates for a rewarding career in sports and athletics as an executive, professional, athlete or entrepreneur. To achieve this, we backwards map our curriculum focus starting with career paths, college options, high school course alignment, as well as middle school critical and conceptual development."

"[Sports] offers us [a] real-world framework, a high-interest hook on which to hang our curriculum. . . . . African American boys have the highest at-risk numbers and the highest dropout rates" in Dyett's attendance boundary, Campbell continued: "40 percent of African American [girls] have either a D or F in math. . . . . By a show of hands, how many of you are shocked by these numbers? I mean, let's be real." Campbell also described an in-house sports nutrition café, sports medical facility, and a maker lab where students would apply knowledge from their science classes to run small businesses supervised by professionals.

The final presentation came from Little Black Pearl, a youth arts nonprofit based in Bronzeville. The proposal was introduced by Terri Evans, a member of the organization's board of directors, and Matthew Kupritz, the architect who would design their proposed new facility; the proposal was for the Little Black Pearl School of the Arts, which would offer an integrated arts curriculum. Evans first presented achievement and growth statistics for the two schools Little Black Pearl was already operating. She described the college preparatory curriculum the school would provide and the community and corporate partnerships that would "serve as ambassadors and allies to create opportunities in the arts for students." Next to speak was Kupritz, an architect from the firm that designed Little Black Pearl's existing arts facility, presenting floor plans and renderings. The proposal outlined the resources the new school would include:

"LBP is proposing the acquisition and renovation of Dyett High School, transforming the school facility into one of the greatest arts and culture assets of Chicago. The facility's unique contemporary design will highlight the essence of LBP's new model for education that engages the entire community. The facility will feature an indoor/outdoor state-of-the-arts theater, gallery/exhibition space, glassblowing facility, creative arts incubator spaces, and a skateboard park designed to strategically position the school as an anchor for arts, education, youth employment, and community development."

In this plan, aspects of the school (such as the performance theater) would be available for public use. "Our objective is to enable [the school] to connect back to the park, to connect back to the community" to "reinvigorate" the facility, he explained.

23. The assembled group was more or less divided between WPACA supporters on the right side of the auditorium and Coalition supporters on the left. Many also argued vehemently that the community needed a school that focused first on academics, rather than sports or the arts. "These two proposals are setting our people back. Back to the days of Stepin Fetchit," said one speaker. "And I don't want that. I want to go forward with green technology!" Another speaker, a parent at a nearby elementary school, agreed. "It is an insult to propose sports and entertainment schools for black children. We should have well-rounded sports and arts in a world-class neighborhood school."

Those supporting WPACA pushed back against that interpretation, arguing that the sports framework was just an entry point for a diverse curriculum. "This proposal and this comprehensive effort would equip our young men and women with twenty-first-century skills within the context of preparing them for careers in the diverse industry of athletics and sports," said one speaker. "It is amazing how this industry has grown and continues to grow rapidly." Others reiterated this point while emphasizing the opportunity for socioeconomic mobility that could come from the WPACA plan; one CPS athletics coach stated, "It's time to be more than an athlete down on the field. It's time to be an owner in a box seat." Another speaker argued that CPS should promote the benefits of health and wellness to young people, saying that "if you have a good solid understanding about how to take care of your body earlier in your life, you will appreciate fitness and sports."

24. Three people spoke in support of the Little Black Pearl proposal. "I understand you love your community. But if you do, give Little Black Pearl a chance," said one young woman, sharing her personal experience as a gradu-

ate of one of Little Black Pearl's existing schools. Another, making reference to the criticisms from other speakers, said that "good leadership does not rely on tearing others down" and that the arts would be an effective pathway for reengaging learners who have lost interest in school. A third, a teacher, said that the professional community at the school was like a family, and that the Coalition's proposal didn't include many of the important cultural learning experiences offered to students at Little Black Pearl.

As the evening wore on, the groups became more directly contentious and critical of the process itself. Some speakers criticized the WPACA team for submitting their proposal after the deadline, as had been reported in the newspaper the week before. "This is really about transparency and accountability, because CPS broke its own rules by allowing that proposal to be turned in an hour and fifteen minutes late."

25. Spielman, "City Council Shuffle."

26. Cox, "Ald. Burns."

27. Cholke, "Dyett Supporters Take Over Ald. Will Burns' Meeting."

28. Lutton, "Budget Squeeze."

29. Chicago Public Schools, "Dyett RFP."

30. H. Reich, "Saluting Capt. Walter Dyett, Who Made Starts at DuSable." August 21, 2013, *Chicago Tribune*, retrieved from http://articles.chicagotribune.com/2013-08-21/entertainment/ct-ent-0821-jazz-dusable-20130821_1_walter-dyett-band-gene-ammons.

31. J. Taylor-Ramann, "Why I'm Hunger Striking for Dyett High School," August 24, 2015, *Chicago Reporter*, http://www.chicagoreporter.com/why-im-hunger-striking-for-dyett-high-school/.

32. This prompts an important question. Is this the school plan that most Bronzeville residents would support? The Coalition represented several community voices and long-term engagement, but does that mean a majority of people within the attendance area would be in favor of the plan? This question highlights a fundamental problem with the governance structure of Chicago schools—there is no real way of knowing, because there are virtually no opportunities for most people to express a democratic preference for one proposal or another. For instance, we might imagine a referendum vote held in the ward—but the ward, a city legislative designation, doesn't map precisely onto school attendance boundaries. Currently, CPS's primary methods for soliciting broad community feedback are board meetings and public hearings, neither of which allows a binding or comprehensive base of perspectives in the way that a vote does. But did most parents in the attendance boundary want this proposal? Or know about it? We can't say, and that is symptomatic of a much larger issue.

33. Negovan, "CPS Announces."

34. Chicago Public Schools, "CPS Announces New Dyett."

35. "Chicago Hunger Strikers."

36. Ford, "Anna Jones."
37. empathyeducates, *Dyett Hunger Strike*.
38. Bell, "Brown v. Board of Education."
39. Cholke, "Dyett Reopens."
40. Eltagouri and Perez, "After Hunger Strike."
41. Lipinski, "Memories."

CHAPTER TWO

1. Vevea and Keefe, "Emanuel Addresses Race."
2. Hatch, "Mass School Closings."
3. Chicago Teachers Union, "President Lewis' Statement."
4. Krauser, "School Closing Opponents."
5. Chicago Public Schools, *CPS Board of Education Monthly Meeting*.
6. South Park Way is sometimes written as South Parkway.
7. Drake and Cayton, *Black Metropolis*, 379–80.
8. Ibid., 8.
9. Ibid., 9–10.
10. Ibid., 58–59.
11. The commission was established to investigate the causes of the city's 1919 race riot, in which over five hundred Chicagoans were injured, thirty-one were murdered by mobs or vigilantes, and seven black men were killed by police. See Tuttle, *Race Riot*.
12. Chicago Commission on Race Relations, *Negro in Chicago*, 123.
13. Ibid., 125.
14. Ibid., 124.
15. Ibid., 123.
16. Travis, "Bronzeville." Strictly speaking, Bronzeville is not one of Chicago's seventy-seven officially designated "community areas"—that is to say, it's not a neighborhood per se. Comprising two community areas (Douglas and Grand Boulevard), Bronzeville is, as journalist Natalie Moore has noted, "a social construction," reflecting boundaries rooted in shared culture and shared struggle. For my analysis, I define the community as bounded by 51st Street on the south, Cermak on the north, Cottage Grove on the east, and State Street on the west.
17. Jones-Correa, "Origins and Diffusion," 559.
18. Hirsch, "Restrictive Covenants."
19. Pattillo, *Black on the Block*, 34.
20. Brooks, "Covenants and Conventions," 12.
21. Jones-Correa, "Origins and Diffusion," 559.
22. Commission on Chicago Landmarks, "Black Metropolis."
23. Lipsitz, *How Racism Takes Place*, 52.
24. Ibid.

25. Ibid.

26. Wright, *12 Million Black Voices*, 104–6.

27. Wirth and Bernert, *Local Community Fact Book of Chicago*.

28. Rosskam, "In the 'Kitchenette' Area."

29. Fuerst, *When Public Housing Was Paradise*, 42.

30. Oscar C. Brown Sr. (father of the renowned performer and activist of the same name) was appointed as the first manager of Ida B. Wells. In an oral history, he describes how he used principles of collective responsibility in his approach to tenant management: "The social work people thought that we should take each tenant separately and tell them how to behave. I said, 'I won't do it that way. I'll take the tenants from each building and have a conference with all of them and say, 'Here's what we are supposed to do.' . . . So I said, 'You've contracted among yourselves that we will make a success of this thing.' That's how I did it." Brown instituted flower competitions, brought medical services to Ida B. Wells, and sent out congratulatory newsletters highlighting residents who were contributing positively to the community. See Fuerst, *When Public Housing Was Paradise*, 11.

31. Hunt, *Blueprint for Disaster*, 45. This preoccupation with cost came partially to meet the constraints of Nathan Straus, a wealthy philanthropist who had been appointed as head of the United States Housing Authority. Straus was passionate about proving that the government could effectively house citizens at lower cost than the private market and was motivated to encourage cost-cutting that resulted in the signature bare-bones architecture that has made public housing projects so identifiable in the American consciousness. "There will be no frills in any housing projects," he announced in a 1938 speech to a group of architects, and "all unnecessary features will be eliminated from any plans submitted." See Hunt, *Blueprint for Disaster*, chap. 2.

32. Fuerst, *Public Housing*, 15–16.

33. Hunt, *Blueprint for Disaster*, 55. Wood's fear was far from unfounded. In 1947, white mobs infuriated that eight black families had moved into the CHA's Fernwood Homes (an eighty-seven-unit housing project intended for veterans, in the Roseland neighborhood) initiated mass rioting. The violence lasted four nights and brought out over a thousand police officers to quell it. In 1953 Betty Howard, a light-skinned African American woman, was assigned housing in the all-white Trumbull Park Homes; when her family moved in and neighbors recognized them as black, white mobs set off explosives and broke windows at their home until the family required police escorts to leave the house (Hunt, *Blueprint for Disaster*, 102). Any hope that CHA projects might be integrated evaporated when, in 1954, Wood was fired in favor of William Kean, a former Korean War brigadier general; many other CHA officials resigned to protest her departure. Emil Hirsch, who worked in public relations in the agency from 1942 to 1955, recounts the change this way: "I think the city fathers, as part of a compromise with the people who were opposed to the whole program [of public

housing], must have made a deal and said, 'We'll get rid of Elizabeth Wood and the people supporting her if you won't kill the whole program.' . . . The people who were really concerned about the welfare of the tenants were replaced by a staff that saw this as a nine-to-five job. We had tried to maintain some sort of integration of the projects in the face of a mounting black application list. When [Wood's] successor, Kean, was confronted with this huge buildup of black applications, he handled it just the way an army general would." See Fuerst, *Public Housing*, 21–22.

34. Hunt, *Blueprint for Disaster*, 110.

35. *Gautreaux v. Chicago Housing Authority*.

36. Hunt, *Blueprint for Disaster*, 132.

37. Ibid., 150.

38. In *Blueprint for Disaster*, Hunt makes an interesting case that these proportions were the root cause of social disorder in Chicago's public housing—not the more widely presumed cause, high-rise architecture. Hunt's analyses of the ratios between young people and adults inspired me to make a similar analysis of the ratio between school-age children and adults in an earlier version of this book.

39. Hunt, *Blueprint for Disaster*, 162.

40. Venkatesh, *American Project*, 24.

41. Anderson and Pickering, *Confronting the Color Line*, 49.

42. Ibid., 56.

43. Neckerman, *Schools Betrayed*, 91.

44. This confrontation came in the midst of rapid demographic change in Englewood. The neighborhood's first residents were German and Irish. In 1950 black people made up 11 percent of the population. Just ten years later the neighborhood had almost completely "flipped," and 69 percent of its residents were black. Today the neighborhood is virtually all black, though talk of displacement and gentrification abounds since the opening of a Whole Foods store in 2016 and the announcement that four Englewood high schools will likely be consolidated. See Stockwell, "Englewood."

45. "Pupils' Strike in Englewood," 14.

46. Anderson and Pickering, *Confronting the Color Line*, 61.

47. Rury, "Race, Space, and the Politics of Chicago's Public Schools," 131.

48. Anderson and Pickering, *Confronting the Color Line*, 77. This report was later corroborated by other officially commissioned reports, including the Havighurst report and the Coons report. The recommendations from these various reports, even those called for from within CPS, were not implemented.

49. Anderson and Pickering, *Confronting the Color Line*, 85.

50. Rury, "Race, Space, and the Politics of Chicago's Public Schools," 125.

51. Herrick, *Chicago Schools*, 312.

52. Hunt, *Blueprint for Disaster*, 162.

53. Herrick, *Chicago Schools*, 312.

54. Anderson and Pickering, *Confronting the Color Line*, 89.

55. *Chicago Tonight*, "1963 Chicago Public School Boycott."

56. "School Boycott Collection."

57. Stone, "Stone's Throw," 1.

58. Olbey, Cartoon.

59. Herrick, *Chicago Schools*, 324.

60. "Chicago Has No Ghettos."

61. Rury, "Race, Space, and the Politics of Chicago's Public Schools," 134.

62. Todd-Breland, "'To Reshape and Redefine Our World,'" 12–13.

63. Ibid., 3–4.

64. Rury, "Race, Space, and the Politics of Chicago's Public Schools," 137.

65. Todd-Breland, "'To Reshape and Redefine Our World,'" 44.

66. Flicker, *Justice and School Systems*, 315–16.

67. Orfield, Kucsera, and Siegel-Hawley, "E Pluribus . . . Separation," xvii.

68. Venkatesh, *American Project*, 119.

69. Fuerst, *When Public Housing Was Paradise*, 146.

70. Reardon and Brodt, "Public Housing."

71. Hunt, *Blueprint for Disaster*, 240.

72. Venkatesh, *American Project*, 26.

73. In 1994 the troubles with this high-density construction captured the city's attention after five-year-old Eric Morse was tragically killed. Two other young boys threw him out a fourteenth-story window in the Ida B. Wells Homes after he refused to steal candy for them.

74. "Chicago Housing Agency."

75. Walinsky, "What It's Like."

76. Finally, in 1996 the US Department of Housing and Urban Development (HUD) took control of the CHA out of the city's hands. Under new federal guidelines, the CHA would be required to undergo a "viability assessment" to determine levels of distress present in all its housing developments and calculate the cost of renovation. If the cost of renovation would exceed the cost of providing residents with Section 8 vouchers to find housing in the private market elsewhere, the residence would have to be demolished.

77. Bennett, Smith, and Wright, *Where Are Poor People to Live*, 218.

78. Chicago Housing Authority, "Plan for Transformation."

79. Austen, "Last Tower."

80. Vale and Graves, "Chicago Housing Authority's Plan," 10.

81. Rogal, "Uncertain Prospects."

82. George et al., *Chicago Children and Youth*.

83. Ibid., 22.

84. The Plan for Transformation has been widely debated, lauded, and critiqued by politicians, journalists, and scholars, and its enactment provokes

many questions: Will the CHA ever successfully find new homes for *all* displaced residents? Will moving from the hypersegregated projects present new opportunities for residents, or will they land in communities beset with the same social and economic challenges? Did the Plan lead to a decrease in overall crime or simply disperse crime across the city? These questions, though worthwhile, are beyond the scope of this chapter; my purpose is not to assess the outcomes of the Plan itself. I do, however, contend that the Plan represents both the culmination of a century of racially motivated housing policies and the imperfect response to them.

85. Venkatesh et al., "Chicago Public Housing Transformation," iv.

CHAPTER THREE

1. Except for that of Barbara Byrd-Bennett, the names and other identifiers in this chapter have been changed.

2. See Spring, *American Education*.

3. Amazaki, "School Named for Mayo Brothers."

4. "School Honors Genius Overton."

5. "School Plan Will Not Halt Double Shifts."

6. Additionally, all three schools had their designated independent hearing officers determine that they should *not* be closed but nevertheless ultimately were closed. This is a notable coincidence (I did not select based on this criterion and was not aware of this until my data analysis had begun) and is comparatively unusual—across the city, in only twelve of fifty-three schools did a hearing officer recommend to the CEO that a school stay open.

7. While the "era of accountability" often gets special attention for being beset with this mode of thinking, the influx into educational culture of "efficiency" as a value to be relentlessly pursued dates back further, to the dawn of industrialized American capitalism. See Callahan, *Education and the Cult of Efficiency*.

8. Espeland and Sauder, *Engines of Anxiety*, 1.

9. Participants invoke the social language of a trial (Gee, *Introduction to Discourse Analysis*) in other small moments, such as this interaction between a district attorney and the hearing officer during the Williams hearing:

> **Attorney:** I believe both testimonies were intended to demonstrate how the proposal of the twenty-seven classrooms would be within the range, but we're happy to provide additional information if that's what you would like to see.
>
> **Hearing Officer:** Whatever you want to do, it's your case. Anything else?

10. Koretz, *Measuring Up*, 117–18.

11. Chatters, Taylor, and Jayakody, "Fictive Kinship Relations."

12. See, for instance, Patterson, *Rituals of Blood*, and Spillers, "Mama's Baby."

13. US Department of Labor, "Negro Family" (known as the Moynihan Report).

14. In addition to their assertions about the importance of family and the harm that school closures do to family ties, some students, school personnel, and community members outwardly reject the narrative presented by the district. Consider this statement by special education teacher Carol Parker:

> I'm still tryna count thirty classrooms. But I can see now that the classroom that I built for my special ed students will be gone. We'll be the closet on the other side of another room. Because that's the only way you're gonna get that many students in that building. Two, three points difference on the ISAT test? Let's take it back even further. We just got on probation. This is our first time here. Our name has never been on a close list. Never been on a close list. And all of a sudden we're closed!

Here Parker challenges several aspects of the district's narrative—not by disagreeing with the facts as presented, but by questioning whether they should be the basis for a decision. She shifts from using "classroom" as a physical site ("I'm still tryna count thirty classrooms") to "classroom" as a shared cultural space ("the classroom that I built for my special ed students"), then challenges whether the enrollment efficiency range is really the way to ensure an "ideal" classroom arrangement (by suggesting that the numbers Meadows presented will not be feasible unless some students are seated in closets). Parker then suggests that ISAT points, not value-added measures, should determine whether a school stays open, and that the school's history or its consistency with high academic performance, rather than a snapshot view, should be taken into consideration. At Williams, special education teacher Marcia Radmore raises similar concerns.

"What was not taken into consideration was that of the eight rooms, three are used for special education instruction. Within the guidelines of the state and the union contract, special education teachers can have a maximum of fifteen students *with* an aide in the classroom. This means that the three rooms combined have a maximum capacity for forty-five students, not ninety as indicated in the plan. . . . The plan also indicated that the Williams Prep has been on probation for five years. . . . This is incorrect. Our first year of probation began in school year 2010–11. We were listed as academic warning year one. Since then our school has not received any additional supports for our teachers and our students to use to improve our students' academic performance."

In addition to challenging the method used to calculate available space and arguing that the record presented of Williams's academic history includes an error, Radmore is also implying that it is not only the school that should face a quality assessment and culpability for low academic performance, but also the district; what is relevant is not only that the school faced academic warning, but also that CPS did not offer any resources or a pathway for improvement.

15. Ravitch, "Same Old Miracle School."

16. See Stovall, *Born out of Struggle*.

17. Although Chicago's school closings are often referred to as targeting "students of color," in fact Latino schools were not overrepresented in those slated for closure.

18. Buelow, "Provident Hospital."

19. "Derrion Albert's Death."

20. The Olympic bid was presaged by the announcement of the "Mid-South Plan," an integrated effort led by myriad entities ranging from the Department of Transportation to the Chicago Housing Authority to the mayor's office to transform a subarea of Bronzeville into one more desirable and more connected to the city as a whole. Critics argued that the Mid-South Plan was an intentional, coordinated effort to push out poor black residents in order to attract wealthier people. See City of Chicago Department of Planning and Development, "Reconnecting Neighborhoods Plan," and Dell'Angela, "South Side Faces School Shake-up."

21. Lipman, *New Political Economy*.

22. Ibid., 11.

CHAPTER FOUR

1. The school once known as Douglas Elementary sits on land with an interesting and troubling history, suggesting it may also be home to ghosts of a different kind. The area was once home to Camp Douglas, which held thousands of Confederate prisoners of war. Even by the standards of the time, the camp was considered especially inhumane and unsanitary. See Knight, "Chicago's Forgotten Civil War Prison Camp." Thanks to John Taylor for telling me about this strange history.

2. Ewing, "Phantoms."

3. I define *institution* as a spatially bound entity or collective enterprise convened for a communal purpose beyond the immediate needs of one individual or family. While many institutions may therefore be publicly owned and operated (a school, a public housing project), this definition also includes privately owned enterprises that, beyond their explicit primary function, serve some secondary communal social function (a barbershop that offers not only haircuts but also a place for community discourse; a corner store that not only sells packaged goods but serves as a gathering place).

4. In *Choosing Homes, Choosing Schools*, Paul Jargowsky puts a finer point on this: "Despite the Fair Housing Act of 1968, despite the emergence of a substantial black middle class, and despite black progress in many professions, the color line remains the primary division in America's neighborhoods. Indeed,

at the pace of the decline in black-white segregation since 1990, it would take 150 years to achieve a low level of segregation ([a dissimilarity index of] 0.30 or less) of blacks from whites" (Jargowsky, "Segregation, Neighborhoods, and Schools").

5. Wilson, *Truly Disadvantaged*, 29.

6. Reardon, Fox, and Townsend, "Neighborhood Income," 85.

7. Dawson, *Black Visions*, 255.

8. Pew Research Center, "On Views of Race."

9. Anft and Lipman, "How Americans Give."

10. Morris, "Pillar of Strength."

11. Hunter, *Black Citymakers*.

12. Laurence Ralph discusses this phenomenon beautifully in an ethnographic account of Mrs. Lana, a black Chicago woman diagnosed as mentally ill by her doctors because she continues to grieve her son, killed by gunfire, at times and in ways deemed unacceptable. Mrs. Lana's refusal to accept that her son is dead earns her a stay in the local jail and a label of delusional. Her neighbors, on the other hand, view her "madness" as normal and reasonable. Further, they use her moments of acute grief as a means of processing their own losses. See Ralph, "Becoming Aggrieved."

13. Laurie and Neimeyer, "African Americans in Bereavement."

14. Horowitz et al., "Diagnostic Criteria."

15. Names are pseudonyms except where participants asked me to use their real names. Names of schools participants are affiliated with have also been changed in this chapter.

16. Hunter et al., "Black Placemaking," 39.

17. A key facet of mourning is that it demands the bereaved reassess their place in the world and their understanding of its functioning, since the loss they have experienced challenges their sense of personal identity and "the underlying structure on which our self-narrative depends . . . on which we rely as our taken-for-granted senses of security, trust, and optimism" (Neimeyer, Prigerson, and Davies, "Mourning and Meaning," 240). In *The Sociology of Teaching*, one of the earliest works in the sociology of education, originally published in 1932, Willard Waller described schools as a "social organism," defined in part by what he referred to as the "we-feeling." This pervasive feeling invites a sense of belonging through which individuals within the institution understand themselves as its component parts. Thus the love the bereaved feel for the lost institution not only is a love *of* the institution but may also be a love for and familiarity with *oneself within* the institution.

18. Ross's description of her and her colleagues' attitude toward their students reflects the trope of the "warm demander" (Kleinfeld, "Effective Teachers"; Ware, "Warm Demander Pedagogy"), the teacher who approaches students of color with equal parts discipline and care, authority and nurturing,

and who engages in the black feminist practice of "othermothering" (Collins, *Black Feminist Thought*).

19. Rosenblatt and Wallace, *African American Grief*, 51.

20. Kauffman, *Shame of Death*.

21. This echoes Johnson's ("'Turnaround'") description of school closure as "shock therapy" and Lipman, Vaughan, and Gutierrez's ("Root Shock") description of their impact as "root shock."

22. Spargo, *Vigilant Memory*, 21.

23. Rosenblatt and Wallace, *African American Grief*, 9.

24. "Table: School Closings Over 10 Years."

25. We also saw this characterization in chapter 3, when one community participant at a closure hearing shouted at district representatives, "Y'all are a gang!"

26. Ralph, *Renegade Dreams*.

27. "Table: School Closings Over 10 Years."

28. See Farmer, *Pathologies of Power*, 8–9.

29. Participants' overall focus on the *way* the loss of their schools occurred is similar to perspectives Deeds and Pattillo heard in their study of a school closure in Newark, New Jersey. "You know, first off, sometimes it's not what you do but how you do it," one teacher told them. "How it was done was just totally wrong . . . and disturbing in the case of teachers. They *are* employees but it's not what you do, it's how you do it" (Deeds and Pattillo, "Organizational 'Failure,'" 487). Fay argues that this perspective is partially a result of the "abnormal justice" inherent in urban school closure: a context where competing entities do not share a common definition of justice; further, Fay argues, community members face *misrepresentation* (being denied real political participation in the process of school closure) and *misrecognition* (feeling disrespected or subordinated). Both misrepresentation and misrecognition are pervasive in the participant accounts ("School Closure and Abnormal Justice").

30. In relating "African American mourning stories," Karla F. Holloway shares reflections on grief, death, and mourning that are intended to illustrate something fundamental about the nature of mortality in black life and thereby something about the nature of the world. "The stories constructed from reflection on these deaths are mourning stories. Their performance constructs a narrative that rehearses the permeability and violence of our culture's racialized boundary conditions. The narratives are imagined in fiction and are improvised in performative community rituals" (Holloway, "Cultural Narratives Passed On").

31. Smith and Stovall, "'Coming Home,'" 140.

32. Ayala and Galletta ("Documenting Disappearing Spaces," 152) write about two school closures as leaving ghostly manifestations in their aftermath: "Despite efforts to erase what once was, afterimages or perhaps ghosts remain

that may manifest themselves most clearly in times of conflict, tension, or community trauma." See also Gordon, *Ghostly Matters*.

33. TEAM Englewood, "Hide Your Schools."

34. Cobb, "Annals of Education."

35. Hunter, *Black Citymakers*, 190.

36. Demby, "What We Lose."

37. Butler, "After Loss, What Then?," 468.

CONCLUSION

1. This brief discussion of "frames" is informed by a variety of scholars who discuss the concept in differing but complementary ways. For a fascinating study of how *collective action* frames shape people's perceptions of and reactions to mass media depictions of political issues, see Gamson, *Talking Politics*.

2. For insights on the use of framing as a form of political agency within black urban communities, see Hunter, *Black Citymakers*.

3. Perez, "Chicago Public Schools Takes Heat."

4. Mbekeani-Wiley, *Handcuffs in Hallways*.

5. Lorde, *Sister Outsider*.

6. Chapter 2 includes Richard Wright's detailed descriptions of Bronzeville's kitchenette buildings. Later in the same book, *12 Million Black Voices*, he describes the devastating weight on the shoulders of migrants coming northward. "[The world] was destined to test all we were, [it] threw us into the scales of competition to weigh our mettle. And how were we to know that, the moment we landless millions of the land—we men who were struggling to be born—set our awkward feet upon the pavements of the city, life would begin to exact of us a heavy toll in death?" (93). Though the four stories described above may seem distinct, they form a continuous arc. What Wright describes is the opening chord of a century-old tale. It began with a promise of something better and the immediate and sustained violation of that promise. Where it will end—where, after death, life persists—remains to be seen.

APPENDIX

1. Lawrence-Lightfoot and Davis, *Art and Science of Portraiture*.

2. Motley himself was something of a social boundary sitter. His biographer refers to him as an "outsider with insider privileges," a black man who was very light-skinned, whose family settled in Chicago before the Great Migration cemented racial borders. His father, a sleeping-car porter, moved the family there in 1894 and they settled in Englewood, which was then a white neighborhood. He studied at the prestigious School of the Art Institute of Chicago—where *Nightlife* now hangs. See Bone and Courage, *Muse in Bronzeville*.

3. Atkinson, "Language That Bears Witness," 23.

4. Ross, *Witnessing and Testifying*.

5. Davis, "Narrating the Mute."

6. Willig, *Introducing Qualitative Research*, 120.

7. Fairclough, *Critical Discourse Analysis*, 18.

8. Freud, *Standard Edition of the Complete Psychological Works*, 14:243.

9. Jasper, "Emotions of Protest."

10. Johnson, "'Turnaround,'" 15.

11. Sexton, "Social Life of Social Death," 17.

12. "CPS to Close a Total of 51 Schools."

13. Kelleher, "Will School Choice Kill Chicago's Neighborhood High Schools?"

14. Johnson, "'Turnaround,'" 245.

15. Ewing, "Phantoms."

16. Lawrence-Lightfoot and Davis, *Art and Science of Portraiture*, xvii.

17. Wilson and Chaddha, "Role of Theory," 551–60.

BIBLIOGRAPHY

Ahmed-Ullah, Noreen. "Greater Bronzeville Buffeted by School Closings." *Chicago Tribune*, January 9, 2012. http://articles.chicagotribune.com/2012-01-09/news/ct-met-cps-bronzeville2-20120109_1_closings-donoghue-elementary-cps-policies.

Amazaki, Barbara. "School Named for Mayo Brothers Aids Parents." *Chicago Tribune*, February 9, 1967. http://archives.chicagotribune.com/1967/02/09/page/101/article/school-named-for-mayo-brothers-aids-parents.

Anderson, Alan B., and George W. Pickering. *Confronting the Color Line: The Broken Promise of the Civil Rights Movement in Chicago*. Athens: University of Georgia Press, 2008.

Anft, M., and H. Lipman. "How Americans Give: Chronicle Study Finds That Race Is a Powerful Influence." *Chronicle of Philanthropy*, May 1, 2003. https://www.philanthropy.com/article/How-Americans-Give/188055#.

Apple, M. W., and J. A. Beane. "Schooling for Democracy." *Principal Leadership* 8, no. 2 (2007): 34–38.

Assata's Daughters. "Defund Police, Dismantle ICE!" Accessed February 16, 2016. http://www.assatasdaughters.org/not1more/.

Atkinson, Yvonne. "Language That Bears Witness: The Black English Oral Tradition in the Works of Toni Morrison." In *The Aesthetics of Toni Morrison: Speaking the Unspeakable*, edited by Marc C. Conner. Jackson: University Press of Mississippi, 2000.

Austen, Ben. "The Last Tower: The Decline and Fall of Public Housing." *Harper's Magazine*, May 7, 2012. http://harpers.org/archive/2012/05/the-last-tower/.

Ayala, Jennifer, and Anne Galletta. "Documenting Disappearing Spaces: Erasure and Remembrance in Two High School Closures." *Peace and Conflict: Journal of Peace Psychology* 18, no. 2 (2012): 149.

Ballard, P. B. "Left-Handedness." *School World* 18, no. 216 (1916): 441–44.

Banas, Casey. "12 Educators Hit Jackpot with Excellence Awards." *Chicago Tribune*, November 15, 1990. http://archives.chicagotribune.com/1990/11/15/page/116/article/12-educators-hit-jackpot-with-excellence-awards.

Bell, Derrick. *And We Are Not Saved: The Elusive Quest for Racial Justice*. New York: Basic Books, 2008.

———. "Brown v. Board of Education and the Interest-Convergence Dilemma." *Harvard Law Review* 93 (1980): 518–33.

Bennett, Larry, Janet L. Smith, and Patricia A. Wright. *Where Are Poor People to Live? Transforming Public Housing Communities*. New York: Routledge, 2015.

Berliner, David. "The Near Impossibility of Testing for Teacher Quality." *Journal of Teacher Education* (2005): 205–13.

Berliner, David, and Bruce Biddle. *The Manufactured Crisis: Myths, Fraud, and the Attack on America's Public Schools*. New York: Basic Books, 1995.

The Black Metropolis-Bronzeville District. Chicago: Commission on Chicago Landmarks, 1997. http://www.cityofchicago.org/dam/city/depts/zlup/Historic_Preservation/Publications/Black_Metropolis_Bronzeville.PDF.

Bobo, Lawrence, James R. Kluegel, and Ryan A. Smith. "Laissez-Faire Racism: The Crystallization of a Kinder, Gentler, Antiblack Ideology." In *Racial Attitudes in the 1990s: Continuity and Change*, edited by Steven A. Tuch and Jack K. Martin, 15–42. Westport, CT: Praeger, 1997.

Bone, Robert, and Richard A. Courage. *The Muse in Bronzeville: African American Creative Expression in Chicago, 1932–1950*. New Brunswick, NJ: Rutgers University Press, 2011.

Bonilla-Silva, Eduardo. "What Is Racism? The Racialized Social System Framework." In *White Supremacy and Racism in the Post-Civil Rights Era*, edited by Eduardo Bonilla-Silva, 21–58. Boulder, CO: Lynne Rienner, 2001.

Boyatzis, Richard E. *Transforming Qualitative Information: Thematic Analysis and Code Development*. Thousand Oaks, CA: Sage, 1998.

"Brizard: Some Schools Are Too 'Far Gone' to Save." *CBS Local*, December 1, 2011. http://chicago.cbslocal.com/2011/12/01/brizard-some-schools-are-too-far-gone-to-save/.

Brooks, Gwendolyn. *Blacks*. Chicago: Third World Press, 1992.

Brooks, Richard R. W. "Covenants and Conventions." Research Paper, Northwestern University, 2002. http://papers.ssrn.com/sol3/papers.cfm?abstract_id=353723.

Buelow, Paul A. "Provident Hospital." In *The Encyclopedia of Chicago*, edited by James R. Grossman, Ann Durkin Keating, and Janice L. Reiff. Chicago: University of Chicago Press, 2004. http://www.encyclopedia.chicagohistory.org/pages/1017.html.

Burris, Alexandria. "Caddo Proposes Building Three, Closing Six Schools." *Shreveport Times*, December 18, 2014. http://www.shreveporttimes.com/story/news/education/k-12/2014/12/18/caddo-schools-proposes-building-three-closing-six-schools/20569847/.

Butler, Judith. "After Loss, What Then?" Afterword. In *Loss: The Politics of Mourning*, edited by David L. Eng and David Kazanjian, 467–73. Berkeley: University of California Press, 2003.

Byrne, John, Juan Perez Jr., and Hal Dardick. "Emanuel Wants to Add a CPS Graduation Requirement: Get Acceptance Letter." *Chicago Tribune*, April 5, 2017. http://www.chicagotribune.com/news/local/politics/ct-rahm-emanuel-high-school-requirement-met-20170405-story.html.

Calhoun, Craig. "Why Historical Sociology?" Afterword. In *The Handbook of Historical Sociology*, edited by G. Delanty and E. F. Isin, 383–93. Thousand Oaks, CA: Sage, 2003.

Callahan, Raymond E. *Education and the Cult of Efficiency: A Study of the Forces That Have Shaped the Administration of the Public Schools*. Chicago: University of Chicago Press, 2010.

Center for Research on Education Outcomes (CREDO). *Lights Off: Practice and Impact of Closing Low-Performing Schools*. Stanford, CA: CREDO, 2017. https://credo.stanford.edu/closure-virtual-control-records.

Chatters, Linda M., Robert Joseph Taylor, and Rukmalie Jayakody. "Fictive Kinship Relations in Black Extended Families." *Journal of Comparative Family Studies* 25, no. 3 (1994): 297–312.

Chicago Commission on Race Relations. *The Negro in Chicago: A Study of Race Relations and a Race Riot.* Chicago: University of Chicago Press, 1922. https://archive.org/details/negroinchicagost00chic.

"Chicago Has No Ghettos, Mayor Says." *Chicago Tribune*, July 23, 1963, 4.

"Chicago Housing Agency Called One of Worst in U.S." *Washington Post*, March 18, 1982. http://www.washingtonpost.com/archive/politics/1982/03/18/chicago-housing-agency-called-one-of-worst-in-us/14942fc9-c85e-401d-a536-53e494e58f49.

Chicago Housing Authority. *Annual Statistical Report 1950*. Chicago: Chicago Housing Authority, 1950.

———. *Annual Statistical Report—June 30, 1960*. Chicago: City of Chicago, Reports and Statistics Division, 1960.

———. "Plan for Transformation." Last modified 2017. http://www.thecha.org/about/plan-for-transformation/.

"Chicago Hunger Strikers Enter Day 19 Challenging Rahm Emanuel's Push to Privatize Public Schools." *Democracy Now!*, September 4, 2015. http://www.democracynow.org/2015/9/4/chicago_hunger_strikers_enter_day_19.

Chicago Public Schools. Chicago Public Schools. Chicago: Chicago Public Schools, 2011. https://www.cityofchicago.org/content/dam/city/narr/Transition%20Reports/PublicSchools.pdf.

———. "CPS Announces New Dyett High School, Innovation Lab." Chicago Public Schools press release, September 3, 2015. Chicago Public Schools website. http://cps.edu/News/Press_releases/Pages/PR1_09_03_2015.aspx.

———. *CPS Board of Education Monthly Meeting April 3, 2013, Part 1*. Filmed April 2013. YouTube video, 42:43. Posted April 9, 2017. http://www.youtube.com/watch?v=sINJ_gwNdvM.

———. "Dyett RFP Process Extended to Provide Adequate Time to Review Community Feedback and Proposals." Chicago Public Schools press release, August 7, 2015. Chicago Public Schools website. http://cps.edu/News/Press_releases/Pages/PR1_8_7_2015.aspx.

———. *LSC Elections 2016*. Last modified 2017. http://cps.edu/ScriptLibrary/Map-LSCElections2016/index.html.

———. *School Data*. Excel files, downloaded and archived. http://cps.edu/SchoolData/Pages/SchoolData.aspx. Accessed January 12, 2016; last modified 2017.

———. *Success Starts Here: Three-Year Vision, 2016–2019*. Last modified 2017. http://cps.edu/Pages/AboutCPS.aspx.

Chicago Southside Principal. "A Common Sense Plea." In *Chicago Principals Reporter* 58, no. 1 (1968): 11–27.

Chicago Teachers Union. "President Lewis' Statement on School Closings." CTU Communications, March 21, 2013. http://www.ctunet.com/blog/ctu-president-karen-lewis-statement-on-cps-school-closings.

Chicago Tonight. "1963 Chicago Public School Boycott." *WWTW*, October 22, 2013. http://chicagotonight.wttw.com/2013/10/22/1963-chicago-public-school-boycott.

Cholke, Sam. "Dyett Reopens with $14.6M Upgrade a Year after Hunger Strike Stops Closure." *DNAinfo*, September 1, 2016. https://www.dnainfo.com/chicago/20160901/grand-boulevard/dyett-reopens-with-146m-upgrade-year-after-hunger-strike-stops-closure.

———. "Dyett Supporters Take Over Ald. Will Burns' Meeting on Saving the School." *DNAinfo*, July 29, 2014. https://www.dnainfo.com/chicago/20140729/kenwood/dyett-supporters-take-over-ald-will-burns-meeting-on-saving-school.

Cholo, Ana Beatriz. "Little Village Getting School It Hungered For." *Chicago Tribune*, February 27, 2005. http://articles.chicagotribune.com/2005-02-27/news/0502270311_1_hunger-strike-chicago-public-schools-schools-chief-arne-duncan.

City of Chicago. "Mayor Emanuel Lays Out Comprehensive Plan to Address CPS Budget Crisis, Warns of Deeper Cuts." City of Chicago press release, July 1, 2015. City of Chicago website. http://www.cityofchicago.org/city/en/depts/mayor/press_room/press_releases/2015/july/mayor-emanuel-lays-out-comprehensive-plan-to-address-cps-budget-.html.

City of Chicago Department of Planning and Development. "Reconnecting Neighborhoods Plan," 2010. https://www.cityofchicago.org/city/en/depts/dcd/supp_info/reconnecting_neighborhoodsplan.html.

"Clement Hits at Willis on TV Program." *Chicago Tribune*, March 7, 1966.

Coalition to Revitalize Walter H. Dyett High School. "Walter H. Dyett Global Leadership and Green Technology High School." Chicago Public Schools proposal, April 6, 2015. http://cps.edu/SiteCollectionDocuments/DyettRFP_DyettGlobalAndGreenTechnologyHSProposal.pdf.

Cobb, Jelani. "Annals of Education—Class Notes: What's Really at Stake When a School Closes?" *New Yorker*, August 31, 2015. http://www.newyorker.com/magazine/2015/08/31/class-notes-annals-of-education-jelani-cobb.

Collins, Patricia Hill. *Black Feminist Thought: Knowledge, Consciousness, and the Politics of Empowerment*. New York: Routledge, 2002.

Commission on Chicago Landmarks. "The Black Metropolis-Bronzeville District." Commission on Chicago Landmarks, 1997. https://www.cityofchicago.org/dam/city/depts/zlup/Historic_Preservation/Publications/Black_Metropolis_Bronzeville.PDF.

Cox, Ted. "Ald. Burns Blocks Charter Resolution Supported by 42 Aldermen." *DNAinfo*, October 5, 2015. https://www.dnainfo.com/chicago/20151005/downtown/ald-burns-blocks-charter-resolution-backed-by-42-aldermen.

"CPS to Close a Total of 51 Schools, 63 Buildings." *CBS Local*, March 21, 2013. http://chicago.cbslocal.com/2013/03/21/cps-begins-informing-schools-of-closing-plans/.

Cram, Robert, "Jones Blasts Segregation in Chicago Public Schools." *Chicago* Defender, September 27, 1958.

Davies, Bronwyn, and Rom Harré. "Positioning: The Discursive Production of Selves." *Journal for the Theory of Social Behaviour* 20, no. 1 (1990): 43–63.

Davis, Dana-Ain. "Narrating the Mute: Racializing and Racism in a Neoliberal Moment." *Souls* 9, no. 4 (2007): 346–60.

Dawson, Michael. *Black Visions: The Roots of Contemporary African-American Political Ideologies*. Chicago: University of Chicago Press, 2003.

Deeds, Vontrese, and Mary Pattillo. "Organizational 'Failure' and Institutional Pluralism: A Case Study of an Urban School Closure." *Urban Education* 50, no. 4 (2015): 474–504.

Dell'Angela, Tracy. "South Side Faces School Shake-Up: Residents Skeptical of City's Plan." *Chicago Tribune*, July 12, 2004. http://articles.chicagotribune.com/2004-07-12/news/0407120194_1_school-reform-chicago-public-schools-schools-chief-arne-duncan/2.

De la Torre, Marisa, Molly F. Gordon, Paul Moore, and Jennifer Cowhy. *School Closings in Chicago: Understanding Families' Choices and Constraints for New School Enrollment*. Chicago: University of Chicago Consortium on Chicago School Research, 2015.

De la Torre, Marisa, and Julia Gwynne. *When Schools Close: Effects on Displaced Students in Chicago Public Schools*. Chicago: University of Chicago Consortium on Chicago School Research, 2009.

Demby, Gene. "What We Lose When a Neighborhood School Goes Away." *NPR*, September 14, 2015. http://www.npr.org/sections/codeswitch/2015/09/14/439450644/what-else-we-lose-when-a-neighborhood-school-goes-away.

"Derrion Albert's Death May Be Rooted in School Closures." NBC Chicago, October 6, 2009. http://www.nbcchicago.com/news/local/holder-arne-duncan-fenger-city-hall-daley-63642507.html.

Dewey, John. *Democracy and Education*. Radford, VA: Wilder, 2008.

Dixson, Adrienne. "Whose Choice? A Critical Race Perspective on Charter Schools." In *The Neoliberal Deluge: Hurricane Katrina, Late Capitalism, and the Remaking of New Orleans*, edited by Cedric Johnson, 130–51. Minneapolis: University of Minnesota Press, 2011.

"'Don't Boo. Vote': Barack Obama's 2016 Democratic Convention Speech in Full." *Guardian*, July 28, 2016. https://www.theguardian.com/us-news/2016/jul/28/dont-boo-vote-barack-obamas-2016-democratic-convention-speech-in-full.

Drake, St. Clair, and Horace R. Cayton. *Black Metropolis: A Study of Negro Life in a Northern City.* 3rd ed. Chicago: University of Chicago Press, 1970.

Du Bois, W. E. B. *Darkwater: Voices from within the Veil*. New York: Harcourt, Brace, and Howe, 1920.

———. *The Souls of Black Folk*. Chicago: A. C. McClurg, 1903.

Eltagouri, Marwa, and Juan Perez Jr. "After Hunger Strike, Dyett Reopens as Arts-Focused Neighborhood High School." *Chicago Tribune*, September 6, 2016, http://www.chicagotribune.com/news/ct-dyett-high-school-reopening-met-20160906-story.html.

"Emanuel Says Quazzo Should Remain on Board of Ed Despite Financial Interests." *Chicago Sun-Times*, June 24, 2016. http://chicago.suntimes.com/news/emanuel-says-quazzo-should-remain-on-board-of-ed-despite-financial-interests/.

empathyeducates. *Dyett Hunger Strike Post Strike Press Conference*. YouTube video, 5:08. Posted September 22, 2015. http://www.youtube.com/watch?v=pZSpKy-RWc0.

Espeland, Wendy, and Michael Sauder. *Engines of Anxiety: Academic Rankings, Reputation, and Accountability.* New York: Russell Sage Foundation, 2016.

Ewing, Eve L. "Phantoms Playing Double-Dutch: Why the Fight for Dyett Is Bigger Than One Chicago School Closing." *Seven Scribes*, August 26, 2015. http://sevenscribes.com/phantoms-playing-double-dutch-why-the-fight-for-dyett-is-bigger-than-one-chicago-school-closing/.

Fairclough, Norman. *Critical Discourse Analysis: The Critical Study of Language*. New York: Longman Group, 1995.

Farmer, Paul. *Pathologies of Power: Health, Human Rights, and the New War on the Poor*. Berkeley: University of California Press, 2003.

Fay, Jacob. "School Closure and Abnormal Justice." PhD diss., Harvard University, 2015.

Feldman, Roberta M., and Susan Stall. *The Dignity of Resistance: Women Residents' Activism in Chicago Public Housing*. New York: Cambridge University Press, 2011.

Fitzpatrick, Lauren. "After Its Own Deadline, CPS Permits Third Proposal for Dyett HS—a Sports-Themed School." *Chicago Sun-Times*, June 8, 2015. http://chicago.suntimes.com/news/7/71/672506/cps-permits-third-proposal-dyett-hs-deadline-sports-themed-hs.

Flicker, Barbara. *Justice and School Systems: The Role of the Courts in Education Litigation*. Philadelphia: Temple University Press, 2011.

Ford, Anne. "Anna Jones: The Hunger Striker." *Chicago Reader*, December 9, 2015. http://people2015.chicagoreader.com/who/anna-jones/profile/.

Fortino, Ellyn. "Chicago Education Activists Launch Coalition to Revitalize Bronzeville's Dyett High School." *Progress Illinois*, November 22, 2013. http://progressillinois.com/quick-hits/content/2013/11/22/chicago-education-activists-launch-coalition-revitalize-bronzevilles-d.

———. "UIC Education Experts: Chicago Should Move to an Elected School Board." *Progress Illinois*, February 19, 2015. http://www.progressillinois.com/posts/content/2015/02/19/uic-researchers-chicago-should-move-elected-school-board.

Foucault, Michel. *The Foucault Reader*. New York: Pantheon Books, 1984.

Fournier, Holly. "'Give Our District a Chance': Rally Fights DPS Closings." *Detroit News*, February 17, 2017. http://www.detroitnews.com/story/news/local/detroit-city/2017/02/17/school-rally/98035742/.

Freud, Sigmund, Anna Freud, Angela Richards, Carrie Lee Rothgeb, and James Strachey. *The Standard Edition of the Complete Psychological Works. Translated from the German Under the General Editorship of James Strachey, in Collaboration with Anna Freud*. London: Hogarth Press and the Institute of Psycho-analysis, 1974.

Fuerst, J. S. *When Public Housing Was Paradise: Building Community in Chicago*. Urbana: University of Illinois Press, 2005.

Gallagher, Charles A. "Color-Blind Privilege: The Social and Political Functions of Erasing the Color Line in Post Race America." *Race, Gender and Class* 10, no. 4 (2003): 22–37.

Gamson, William A. *Talking Politics. Cambridge: Cambridge University Press, 1992.*

Gee, James Paul. *An Introduction to Discourse Analysis: Theory and Method*, 4th ed. New York: Routledge, 2014.

George, Robert, John Dilts, Duck-itye Yang, Miriam Wasserman, and Anne Clary. *Chicago Children and Youth 1990–2010: Changing Population Trends and Their Implications for Services*. Chicago: Chapin Hall Center for Children at the University of Chicago, 2007.

Golab, Art. "Referendum on Elected School Board Nets 83% to 93% Yes Votes in 37 Wards." *Chicago Sun-Times*, June 24, 2016. http://chicago.suntimes.com/politics/referendum-on-elected-school-board-nets-83-to-93-yes-votes-in-37-wards/.

Gordon, Avery. *Ghostly Matters: Haunting and the Sociological Imagination*. Minneapolis: University of Minnesota Press, 2008.

Granger, David. "No Child Left Behind and the Spectacle of Failing Schools: The Mythology of Contemporary School Reform." *Educational Studies: Journal of the American Educational Studies Association* 43, no. 3 (2008): 206–28.

Great Cities Institute. "Why These Schools? Explaining School Closures in Chicago, 2000–2013." University of Illinois at Chicago, November 2016. https://greatcities.uic.edu/wp-content/uploads/2017/01/School-Closure.pdf.

Griffin, Aquila, et al. "Aquila Griffin et al. to Arne Duncan and Russlynn Ali." *EdWeek*, May 8, 2012. http://www.edweek.org/media/dyett_title_vi_letter.pdf.

Hatch, Marshall. "Mass School Closings Hurt Chicago's Poor Children." Austin Weekly News, March 26, 2013. http://www.austinweeklynews.com/News/Articles/3-26-2013/Mass-school-closings-hurt-Chicago's-poor-children/.

Helgeson, Jeffrey. "Fight School Segregation!" *Chicago Urban League Archives*, 2007. http://www.uic.edu/depts/lib/specialcoll/services/rjd/CULExhibit/Urban%20League%20\Exhibit/3_1_Freedom%20Day%20Flyer.htm.

Herrick, Mary J. *The Chicago Schools: A Social and Political History*. Beverly Hills, CA: Sage, 1970.

Hirsch, Arnold R. "Restrictive Covenants." In *The Encyclopedia of Chicago*, edited by James R. Grossman, Ann Durkin Keating, and Janice L. Reiff. Chicago: University of Chicago Press, 2004. http://www.encyclopedia.chicagohistory.org/pages/1067.html.

Holland, Dorothy, William Lachicotte Jr., Debra Skinner, and Carole Cain. *Identity and Agency in Cultural Worlds*. Cambridge, MA: Harvard University Press 1998.

Holloway, K. F. "Cultural Narratives Passed On: African American Mourning Stories. *College English* 59, no. 1 (1997): 32–40.

hooks, bell. *Teaching to Transgress: Education as the Practice of Freedom*. New York: Routledge, 1994.

———. *A Woman's Mourning Song*. New York: Harlem River Press, 1993.

Horowitz, M. J., B. Siegel, A. Holen, G. A. Bonanno, C. Milbrath, and C. H. Stinson. "Diagnostic Criteria for Complicated Grief Disorder." *Focus*, 1, no. 3 (2003): 290–98.

Hunt, D. Bradford. *Blueprint for Disaster: The Unraveling of Chicago Public Housing*. Chicago: University of Chicago Press, 2009.

Hunter, Marcus Anthony. *Black Citymakers: How the Philadelphia Negro Changed Urban America*. New York: Oxford University Press, 2013.

Hunter, Marcus Anthony, Mary Pattillo, Zandria F. Robinson, and Keeanga-Yamahtta Taylor. "Black Placemaking: Celebration, Play, and Poetry." *Theory, Culture and Society* 33, no. 7–8 (2016): 31–56.

Inns, Alicia. "Some AISD Schools May Shut Down due to Conditions, Enrollment." *KXAN*, December 1, 2016. http://kxan.com/2016/12/01/some-aisd-schools-may-shut-down-due-to-bad-conditions/.

Jargowsky, Paul A. "Segregation, Neighborhoods, and Schools." In *Choosing Homes, Choosing Schools: Residential Segregation and the Search for a Good*

School, edited by Annette Lareau and Kimberly Goyette, 97–136. New York: Russell Sage Foundation, 2014.

Jasper, James M. "The Emotions of Protest: Affective and Reactive Emotions in and around Social Movements." *Sociological Forum* 13, no. 3 (1998): 397–424.

Johnson, Amanda Walker. "'Turnaround' as Shock Therapy: Race, Neoliberalism, and School Reform." *Urban Education* 48, no. 2 (2013): 232–56.

Jones-Correa, M. "The Origins and Diffusion of Racial Restrictive Covenants." *Political Science Quarterly* 115, no. 4 (2000): 541–68.

Joravsky, Ben. "Waiting for the Day of Judgment from Mayor Emanuel." *Chicago Reader*, March 3, 2013. http://www.chicagoreader.com/chicago/rahm-emanuel-cps-school-closings-list-utilization/Content?oid=8964005.

Karp, S. "CPS Reverses Course, Says Dyett to Reopen in 2016 as Neighborhood High School." *Catalyst Chicago*, October 24, 2014. Retrieved from http://catalyst-chicago.org/2014/10/cps-reverses-course-says-dyett-reopen-in-2016-neighborhood-high-school/.

———. "Neighborhood High Schools Losing Students." *Catalyst Chicago*, December 20, 2011. http://catalyst-chicago.org/2011/12/neighborhood-high-schools-losing-students/.

Kauffman, Jeffrey, ed. *The Shame of Death, Grief, and Trauma*. New York: Routledge, 2010.

Kelleher, Maureen. "The Changing Face of CPS Teachers." *Chicago Reporter*, September 11, 2015. http://chicagoreporter.com/the-changing-face-of-cps-teachers/.

———. "Chicago Schools: 'Worst in the Nation'?" *Chicago Reporter*, November 13, 2015. http://chicagoreporter.com/chicago-schools-worst-in-the-nation/.

———. "Will School Choice Kill Chicago's Neighborhood High Schools?" *Catalyst Chicago*, October 30, 2015. http://catalyst-chicago.org/2015/10/will-school-choice-kill-chicagos-neighborhood-high-schools/.

Kleinfeld, Judith. "Effective Teachers of Eskimo and Indian Students." *School Review* 83, no. 2 (1975): 301–44.

Knight, Meribah. "Chicago's Forgotten Civil War Prison Camp." *WBEZ*, March 11, 2015. https://www.wbez.org/shows/curious-city/chicagos-forgotten-civil-war-prison-camp/2aea8281-878c-436f-8311-62747b7be31f.

Koretz, Dan. *Measuring Up: What Educational Testing Really Tells Us*. Cambridge, MA: Harvard University Press, 2008.

Krauser, M. "School Closing Opponents Call Mayor a Racist Liar." *CBS Chicago*, March 22, 2013. http://chicago.cbslocal.com/2013/03/22/school-closing-opponents-call-mayor-a-racist-liar.

Kumashiro, Kevin K. *The Seduction of Common Sense: How the Right Has Framed the Debate on America's Schools*. New York: Teachers College Press, 2008.

Lathan, Stan. *Brave New Voices*. Film. HBO.

Lauen, Douglas Lee. "Opportunity for All? The Hidden Causes and Consequences of School Choice in Chicago." PhD diss., University of Chicago, 2006.

Laurie, A., and R. A. Neimeyer. "African Americans in Bereavement: Grief as a Function of Ethnicity." *Omega-Journal of Death and Dying* 57, no. 2 (2008): 173–93.

Lawrence-Lightfoot, Sara, and Jessica Hoffmann Davis. *The Art and Science of Portraiture*. San Francisco: Jossey-Bass, 1997.

Levinson, Meira. *No Citizen Left Behind*. Cambridge, MA: Harvard University Press, 2012.

Lipinski, Ann Marie. "Memories Bring Grand Jazz Back to the School Where It All Began." *Chicago Tribune*, March 21, 1989, sec. 2.

Lipman, Pauline. *The New Political Economy of Urban Education: Neoliberalism, Race, and the Right to the City*. New York: Routledge, 2011.

Lipman, Pauline, and Nathan Haines. "From Accountability to Privatization and African American Exclusion: Chicago's 'Renaissance 2010.'" *Educational Policy* 21, no. 3 (2007): 471–502.

Lipman, Pauline, Kelly Vaughan, and Rhoda Rae Gutierrez. "Root Shock: Parents' Perspectives on School Closings in Chicago." Chicago: Collaborative for Equity and Justice in Education, 2014.

Lipsitz, George. *How Racism Takes Place*. Philadelphia: Temple University Press, 2011.

Little Black Pearl. "CPS Innovative Programmatic Design in Dyett High School." Chicago Public Schools proposal, April 6, 2015. http://cps.edu/SiteCollection Documents/DyettRFP_LittleBlackPearlSchoolOfTheArtsProposal.pdf.

Lorde, Audre. *Sister Outsider: Essays and Speeches*. Berkeley, CA: Crossing Press, 2012.

Lutton, Linda. "Budget Squeeze in Chicago Schools Pushes Some Classes Online." *WBEZ*, July 23, 2013. http://www.wbez.org/news/budget-squeeze-chi cago-schools-pushes-some-classes-online-108158.

Massey, Douglas, and Nancy A. Denton. *American Apartheid: Segregation and the Making of the Underclass*. Cambridge, MA: Harvard University Press, 1993.

Masterson, Matt. "Illinois House Once Again Backs Elected Chicago School Board." *WWTW*, May 25, 2017. http://chicagotonight.wttw.com/2017/05/25 /illinois-house-once-again-backs-elected-chicago-school-board.

Mbekeani-Wiley, Michelle. *Handcuffs in Hallways: The State of Policing in Chicago Public Schools*. Chicago: Sargent Shriver National Center on Poverty Law, 2017. http://povertylaw.org/files/docs/handcuffs-in-hallways-final.pdf.

McGee, Kate. "Austin ISD Parents Prepare for Fight against Possible School Closures." *KUT 90.5*, February 3, 2017. http://kut.org/post/austin-isd-parents -prepare-fight-against-possible-school-closures.

Miller, Alton. *Harold Washington: The Mayor, the Man*. Chicago: Bonus Books, 1989.

Morris, J. E. "A Pillar of Strength: An African American School's Communal Bonds with Families and Community since Brown." *Urban Education* 33, no. 5 (1999): 584–605.

Mullen, W. "The Road to Hell: For Cabrini-Green, It Was Paved with Good Intentions." *Chicago Tribune*, March 31, 1985. http://articles.chicagotribune.com/1985-03-31/features/8501180145_1_cabrini-housing-poverty-and-racism.

Neckerman, Kathryn. *Schools Betrayed: Roots of Failure in Inner-City Education*. Chicago: University of Chicago Press, 2007.

Negovan, Tom. "CPS Announces Dyett Will Be an Open Enrollment School with Arts Focus and Technology Hub." *WGN Chicago*, September 3, 2015. http://wgntv.com/2015/09/03/cps-announces-dyett-will-be-as-open-enrollment-school-with-arts-focus-and-technology-hub/.

Neimeyer, Robert A., Holly G. Prigerson, and Betty Davies. "Mourning and Meaning." American Behavioral Scientist 46, no. 2 (2002): 235–51.

Olbey. Cartoon 1. *Chicago Defender*, national edition, 8. October 12, 1963.

Orfield, G., J. Kucsera, and G. Siegel-Hawley. "E Pluribus… Separation: Deepening Double Segregation for More Students." Los Angeles: Civil Rights Project, UCLA, 2012. http://civilrightsproject.ucla.edu/research/k-12-education/integration-and-diversity/mlk-national/e-pluribus...separation-deepening-double-segregation-for-more-students/orfield_epluribus_revised_omplete_2012.pdf.

Patterson, Orlando. *Rituals of Blood: Consequences of Slavery in Two American Centuries*. Washington, DC: Basic Civitas Books, 1998.

Pattillo, Mary. *Black on the Block: The Politics of Race and Class in the City*. Chicago: University of Chicago Press, 2008.

———. "Everyday Politics of Schools Choice in the Black Community." *Du Bois Journal* 12, no. 1 (2015): 41–71.

Perez, Juan. "Chicago Public Schools Downgrades Four Years of Inflated Graduation Rates." *Chicago Tribune*, October 15, 2015. http://www.chicagotribune.com/news/ct-chicago-school-graduation-rate-change-met-1002-20151001-story.html.

———. "Chicago Public Schools Takes Heat over Special Education Spending Changes." *Chicago Tribune*, December 7, 2016. http://www.chicagotribune.com/news/local/breaking/ct-chicago-schools-special-education-fight-met-20161207-story.html.

Pew Research Center. "On Views of Race and Inequality, Blacks and Whites Are Worlds Apart." June 27, 2016. http://www.pewsocialtrends.org/2016/06/27/1-demographic-trends-and-economic-well-being/.

"Pupils' Strike in Englewood up to Parents." *Chicago Tribune*, September 28, 1945. http://archives.chicagotribune.com/1945/09/28/page/14/article/pupils-strike-in-englewood-up-to-parents.

Ralph, Laurence. "Becoming Aggrieved: An Alternative Framework of Care in Black Chicago." *Russell Sage Foundation Journal of the Social Sciences* 1, no. 2 (2015): 31–41.

———. *Renegade Dreams: Living through Injury in Gangland Chicago*. Chicago: University of Chicago Press, 2014.

Ravitch, Diane. "The Same Old Miracle School in Chicago, with a High Attrition Rate." *Diane Ravitch's Blog*, July 7, 2014. http://dianeravitch.net/2014/07/07/the-same-old-miracle-school-in-chicago-with-a-high-attrition-rate/.

Reardon, Patrick, and Bonita Brodt. "Public Housing Draws the Dividing Line." *Chicago Tribune*, November 30, 1986. http://articles.chicagotribune.com/1986-11-30/news/8603310237_1_chicago-housing-authority-public-housing-chicago-river.

Reardon, Sean F., Lindsay Fox, and Joseph Townsend. "Neighborhood Income Composition by Household Race and Income, 1990–2009." *Annals of the American Academy of Political and Social Science* 660, no. 1 (2015): 78–97.

Roberts, D. E. "Welfare and the Problem of Black Citizenship." *Yale Law Journal* 105 (1996): 1563–1602.

Rogal, B. J. "Uncertain Prospects." *Chicago Reporter*, September 26, 2007. http://chicagoreporter.com/uncertain-prospects/.

Rosenblatt, Paul C., and Beverly R. Wallace. *African American Grief*. New York: Routledge, 2013.

Ross, Rosetta E. *Witnessing and Testifying: Black Women, Religion, and Civil Rights*. Minneapolis, MN: Fortress Press, 2003.

Rosskam, Edwin. "In the 'Kitchenette' Area on South Parkway, a Formerly Well-to-Do Avenue, Chicago, Illinois." Farm Security Administration—Office of War Information Photograph Collection (Library of Congress), April 1941. http://www.loc.gov/item/fsa1997015740/PP.

Rury, John L. "Race, Space, and the Politics of Chicago's Public Schools: Benjamin Willis and the Tragedy of Urban Education." *History of Education Quarterly* 39, no. 2 (1999): 117–42.

Sampson, Robert J. *Great American City: Chicago and the Enduring Neighborhood Effect*. Chicago: University of Chicago Press, 2012.

Saparito, S., and Annette Lareau. "School Selection as a Process: The Multiple Dimensions of Race in Framing Educational Choice." *Social Problems* 46, no. 3 (1999): 418–39.

"School Boycott Collection." Chicago History Museum, Chicago, 2015. http://facingfreedom.org/public-protest/school-boycott/collection.

"School Honors Genius Overton." *Chicago Tribune: South Neighborhood News*, October 7, 1965. http://archives.chicagotribune.com/1965/10/07/page/93/article/school-honors-genius-overton.

"School Plan Will Not Halt Double Shifts." *Chicago Tribune*, April 10, 1952. Retrieved from http://archives.chicagotribune.com/1952/04/10/page/84/article/school-plan-will-not-halt-double-shifts.

Seligman, Amanda. "Community Areas." In *The Encyclopedia of Chicago*, edited by James R. Grossman, Ann Durkin Keating, and Janice L. Reiff. Chicago: University of Chicago Press, 2004. http://www.encyclopedia.chicagohistory.org/pages/319.html.

Sexton, Jared. "The Social Life of Social Death: On Afro-Pessimism and Black Optimism." *InTensions* 5 (2011): 1–47.

Sfondeles, Tina, and Fran Spielman. "Rauner Delivers One School Message in Chicago, Another Downstate." *Chicago Sun-Times*, June 7, 2016. http://chicago.suntimes.com/chicago-politics/gov-rauner-calls-some-cps-schools-are-like-crumbling-prisons/.

Shapiro, Thomas M. *The Hidden Cost of Being African American: How Wealth Perpetuates Inequality*. New York: Oxford University Press, 2004.

Shedd, Carla. *Unequal City: Race, Schools, and Perceptions of Injustice*. New York: Russell Sage Foundation, 2015.

Simon, Stephanie, and James Kelleher. "Should This School Be Saved? The Fight over Chicago's Dyett High." *Chicago Tribune*, November 11, 2012. http://articles.chicagotribune.com/2012-11-11/news/sns-rt-us-education-school-closurebre8aa07i-20121111_1_school-closures-dyett-high-school-jitu-brown.

Sleeter, Christine E. "Preparing White Teachers for Diverse Students." In *Handbook of Research on Teacher Education: Enduring Questions in Changing Contexts*, edited by Marilyn Cochran-Smith, Sharon Feiman-Nemser, D. John McIntyre, and Kelly E. Demers, 559–82. New York: Routledge, 2008.

Smith, Janet L., and David Stovall. "'Coming Home' to New Homes and New Schools: Critical Race Theory and the New Politics of Containment." *Journal of Education Policy* 23, no. 2 (2008): 135–52.

Solórzano, Daniel G., and Tara J. Yosso. "Critical Race Methodology: Counter-Storytelling as an Analytical Framework for Education Research." *Qualitative Inquiry* 8, no. 1 (2002): 23–44.

Spargo, R. Clifton. *Vigilant Memory: Emmanuel Levinas, the Holocaust, and the Unjust Death*. Baltimore: Johns Hopkins University Press, 2006.

Spielman, Fran. "City Council Shuffle Rewards Emanuel Allies." *Chicago Sun-Times*, May 20, 2015. http://chicago.suntimes.com/news/7/71/622429/city-council-sign-reorganization-rewards-emanuel-allies.

Spillers, Hortense J. "Mama's Baby, Papa's Maybe: An American Grammar Book." *Diacritics* 17, no. 2 (1987): 65–81.

Spring, Joel. *American Education*, 18th ed. New York: Routledge, 2018.

Stockwell, Clinton E. "Englewood." In *The Encyclopedia of Chicago*, edited by James R. Grossman, Ann Durkin Keating, and Janice L. Reiff. Chicago: University of Chicago Press, 2004. http://www.encyclopedia.chicagohistory.org/pages/426.html.

Stone, Chuck. "A Stone's Throw." *Chicago Defender*, National Edition 1, October 12, 1963.

Stone, David. "Chicago City Hall Sit-in Day Two: Speakers Outlined Demands of Sit-in as the Famous Fifth Floor of Chicago's City Hall Echoed with the Chants, Prayers, Songs and Spirit of the Civil Rights and Freedom Ride Eras." *Substance News*, January 5, 2012. http://www.substancenews.net/articles.php?page=2968.

Stovall, David Omotoso. *Born out of Struggle: Critical Race Theory, School Creation, and the Politics of Interruption*. Albany: SUNY Press, 2016.

"Table: School Closings Over 10 Years." Catalyst Chicago, December 7, 2011. http://chicagoreporter.com/table-school-closings-over-10-years/.

Taylor, George H. "Derrick Bell's Narratives as Parables." *NYU Review of Law and Social Change* 31 (2006): 225–71.

Taylor-Ramann, Jeanette. "Why I'm Hunger Striking for Dyett High School." *Catalyst Chicago*, August 24, 2015. http://catalyst-chicago.org/2015/08/why-im-hunger-striking-for-dyett-high-school/.

TEAM Englewood, "Hide Your Schools, Hide Your Homes, Hide Your Children, Cause He's Wrecking It All." 2014. https://www.youtube.com/watch?v=OoPAMWSHWPk.

Todd-Breland, Elizabeth. "'To Reshape and Redefine Our World': African American Political Organizing for Education in Chicago, 1968–1988." PhD diss., University of Chicago, 2010.

Travis, Dempsey J. "Bronzeville." In *The Encyclopedia of Chicago*, edited by James R. Grossman, Ann Durkin Keating, and Janice L. Reiff. Chicago: University of Chicago Press, 2004. http://www.encyclopedia.chicagohistory.org/pages/171.html.

Tuttle, William M. Jr. *Race Riot: Chicago in the Red Summer of 1919*. Champaign: University of Illinois Press, 1970.

US Department of Education. *The State of Racial Diversity in the Educator Workforce*. Policy and Program Studies Service, Office of Planning, Evaluation, and Policy Development, 2016. https://www2.ed.gov/rschstat/eval/highered/racial-diversity/state-racial-diversity-workforce.pdf.

US Department of Labor, Office of Policy Planning and Research. "The Negro Family: The Case for National Action" [by Daniel Patrick Moynihan]. March 1965. Available from United States Department of Labor. http://www.dol.gov/dol/aboutdol/history/webid-moynihan.htm.

Vale, L. J., and E. Graves. "The Chicago Housing Authority's Plan for Transformation: What Does the Research Show so Far?" Report to the John D. and Catherine T. MacArthur Foundation, 2010. https://www.macfound.org/media/article_pdfs/VALEGRAVES_CHA_PFT_FINAL-REPORT.PDF.

Venkatesh, Sudhir Alladi. *American Project: The Rise and Fall of a Modern Ghetto*. Cambridge, MA: Harvard University Press, 2002.

Venkatesh, Sudhir, Isil Celimli, Douglas Miller, Alexandra Murphy, and Beauty Turner. *Chicago Public Housing Transformation: A Research Report*. New York:

Center for Urban Research and Policy, Columbia University, 2004. http://www.columbia.edu/cu/curp/publications2/PH_Transformation_Report.pdf.

Vevea, Becky, and Alex Keefe, "Emanuel Addresses Race in Chicago School Closure Plan." WBEZ News, March 27, 2013. https://www.wbez.org/shows/wbez-news/emanuel-addresses-race-in-chicago-school-closure-plan/25b82459-d289-4f95-a4e7-64a4de4b1304.

Walinsky, A. "What It's Like to Be in Hell." *New York Times*, December 4, 1987. http://www.nytimes.com/1987/12/04/opinion/what-it-s-like-to-be-in-hell.html.

Waller, Willard. *The Sociology of Teaching. 1932. Reprinted, Eastford, CT: Martino Fine Books, 2014.*

Ware, Franita. "Warm Demander Pedagogy: Culturally Responsive Teaching That Supports a Culture of Achievement for African American Students." *Urban Education* 41, no. 4 (2006): 427–56.

Washington Park Athletic Career Academy. "Washington Park Athletic Career Academy." Proposal to Chicago Public Schools, 2015. http://cps.edu/SiteCollectionDocuments/DyettRFP_WashingtonParkAcademyProposal.pdf.

Weiner, Mark S. *Black Trials: Citizenship from the Beginnings of Slavery to the End of Caste*. New York: Vintage, 2007.

Whitman Corporation. "Meet Chicago's Best Public School Principals." *Chicago Tribune*, June 28, 1989. http://archives.chicagotribune.com/1989/06/28/page/14/article/display-ad-12-no-title.

Willig, Carla. *Introducing Qualitative Research in Psychology*. New York: McGraw-Hill International, 2013.

Wilson, William Julius. *The Truly Disadvantaged: The Inner City, the Underclass, and Public Policy*. Chicago: University of Chicago Press, 2012.

Wilson, William Julius, and Anmol Chaddha. "The Role of Theory in Ethnographic Research." *Ethnography* 10, no. 4 (2009): 549–64.

Wirth, Louis, and Eleanor H. Bernert. Local Community Factbook of Chicago. Chicago: University of Chicago Press, 1949.

Woodard, D., and Dassie, J. "A Need for Personal Recognition." *Chicago Principals Reporter* 58, no. 1 (1968): 7.

WorldAdmin. "Fighting Back against a School Closing." *KTBS*, March 12, 2011. https://www.ktbs.com/news/fighting-back-against-a-school-closing/article_18bdc7db-6e47-5d25-b3f4-c8725b16286d.html.

Wright, Richard. *12 Million Black Voices. New York: Basic Books, 2008.*

Yosso, Tara J. "Whose Culture Has Capital? A Critical Race Theory Discussion of Community Cultural Wealth." *Race Ethnicity and Education* 8, no. 1 (2005): 69–91.

Ziemba, Stanley. "How Projects Rose to Failure." *Chicago Tribune*, December 2, 1986. http://articles.chicagotribune.com/1986-12-02/news/8603310330_1_chicago-housing-authority-high-rise-projects-public-housing.

INDEX